School-based Mental Health

A Framework for Intervention

Debra S. Lean and Vincent A. Colucci

ROWMAN & LITTLEFIELD EDUCATION

A division of
ROWMAN & LITTLEFIELD PUBLISHERS, INC.
Lanham • New York • Toronto • Plymouth, UK

Published by Rowman & Littlefield Education
A division of Rowman & Littlefield Publishers, Inc.
A wholly owned subsidary of
The Rowman & Littlefield Publishing Group, Inc.
4501 Forbes Boulevard, Suite 200, Lanham, Maryland 20706
www.rowman.com

10 Thornbury Road, Plymouth PL6 7PP, United Kingdom

British Library Cataloguing in Publication Information Available

Library of Congress Cataloging-in-Publication Data

Lean, Debra S. (Debra Susan)
  School-based mental health : a framework for intervention / Debra S. Lean
and Vincent A. Colucci.
     pages cm
  Includes bibliographical references.
  ISBN 978-1-61048-643-9 (cloth : alk. paper) — ISBN 978-1-61048-644-6
(pbk. : alk. paper) — ISBN 978-1-61048-645-3 (electronic) 1. School
children—Mental health services—United States. 2. School psychology—
United States. 3. Clinical psychology—United States. I. Title.
  LB3430.L44 2013
  371.7'130973—dc23   2012040741

∞™ The paper used in this publication meets the minimum requirements of
American National Standard for Information Sciences—Permanence of
Paper for Printed Library Materials, ANSI/NISO Z39.48-1992.

Printed in the United States of America

Contents

Figures and Tables

FIGURES

TABLES

Acronym Guide

CO	Community Organization
CYMH	Child and Youth Mental Health
EBP	Evidence-Based Practice
ESL	English as a Second Language
FTE	Full-Time Equivalent
IDEA	Individuals with Disabilities Education Act
MDT	Multi-Disciplinary Team
MH	Mental Health
MTSS	Multi-Tiered Systems of Support
NASP	National Association of School Psychologists
NASW	National Association of Social Workers
RBA	Results-Based Accountability
SBMH	School-based Mental Health
SCG	School-based Collaboration Group
SCR	School mental health Core Representative
SDMHC	School District Mental Health Committee
SISSM	School-based Integrated Support Services Model
TAC	Team Around the Child

Foreword

In their first book, *Barriers to Learning: The Case for Integrated Mental Health Services in Schools*, Debra Lean and Vincent Colucci systematically made the case for an integrated mental health services model that triangulated schools, mental health services, and the students who would be dramatically better served by such a model. They identified key barriers and indicated the pathways to developing integrated systems that would work effectively. They did not, however, spell out the more detailed aspects of what the new model would look like in practice. This new book, *School-based Mental Health: A Framework for Intervention*, does just that. We get the full package.

For starters, the reader gets a clear re-cap of the existing barriers that stand in the way. But then Lean and Colucci quickly take us into the reality of the current operation of school-based mental health services. We see that the pieces of integration are there, and that they should work in practice, but we also get the feeling that the forces of integration are missing or not strong enough to make it work on a day-to-day basis.

Then we start down the pathway to solutions. The essential components of the model are clearly laid out: the levels of governance, from local to regional to state; capacity building and training; accountability; management of implementation; data support networks; knowledge exchange and learning from implementation; funding mechanisms; and so on. In short, leadership, coordination, collaboration, monitoring, and improvement of practice are all systematically addressed within and across levels.

What is especially significant are the comprehensiveness, clarity, and specificity of both the structures and the knowledge and competencies at the level of all key roles in the education and child-serving sectors. Just to take one aspect—training and support—the authors recommend a combination of embedded professional development paired with ongoing networks, study groups of professional learning communities, alignment with goals and standards, mentoring and coaching during early implementation, and school-level support throughout.

Once the key elements have been identified, the authors provide an array of "tools" that would be used by each school, mapping out school-based needs, personnel required, specific interventions, and overall integrated plans. Most helpfully, all these tools come with complete templates for organizing and storing data. Ideas are presented for identifying concerns, prioritizing needs, and employing interventions to resolve particular problems. Beyond the tools developed by Lean and Colucci are several targeted websites that provide downloadable guides for addressing specific issues.

Having laid out the elements and processes, the authors then devote a chapter to taking us through the actual process of implementing the framework in a sample school district and its schools. In other words, they demonstrate how the framework and its tools work in practice. By this time the readers will be able to see how the framework specifically serves the process of integrating mental health services at the local level.

In sum, the journey through school-based mental health services in this book takes us from barriers to systemic solutions. It is at once comprehensive and specific. The payoff for school and health personnel, and for those whom they serve, is enormous. Those who have been frustrated by unresolved problems and ad hoc interventions now have a solution. Mastering and implementing the framework of intervention will take some work, but it's all there in one place. This book is a goldmine of ideas and tools for integrating school-based mental health services.

Michael Fullan
Professor Emeritus, Ontario Institute for Studies in Education/University of Toronto

Acknowledgments

I would like to thank my coauthor, colleague, and friend, Debra Lean, whose exceptional knowledge of mental health and education and total dedication to quality work have made *School-based Mental Health: A Framework for Intervention* possible. I would like to thank my wonderful family for their encouragement and invaluable support.

I would like to thank my coauthor, colleague, and friend, Vincent Colucci, for his wisdom in all things, particularly the writing process, and his exceptional insight and knowledge regarding school support services. I thank my wonderful family for their support, interest, and encouragement.

Together, we thank Tom Koerner, our editor, and his team at Rowman & Littlefield Education, for their support, guidance, and patience with *School-based Mental Health*, as well as with our first book, *Barriers to Learning: The Case for Integrated Mental Health Services in Schools*.

We also thank Michael Fullan for providing us with thoughtful and enlightened forewords for both of our books.

We sincerely appreciate the support and interest of our friends and colleagues throughout the writing of both books.

We dedicate *School-based Mental Health: A Framework for Intervention* to our spouses and children, Leslie, Lee, and Emma Colucci and Martin, Paul, and Jay Ginsherman.

Vincent A. Colucci   *Debra S. Lean*
August 8, 2012

Introduction

A number of approaches are presently being utilized in the United States, Canada, and internationally in an effort to address the mental health needs of children and youth in schools. Integrating trained and experienced mental health professionals from various community institutions into schools appears to be one of the most commonly discussed practices, and one that continues to be further advanced and developed.

In our first book, *Barriers to Learning: The Case for Integrated Mental Health Services in Schools*, we made the case for the need to provide child and youth mental health services in schools. We recommended that many of these services be provided by school-based district-employed mental health professionals. We introduced the School-based Integrated Support Services Model (SISSM), a model of service delivery designed to effectively integrate professionals and interventions from community organizations into school systems to provide mental health services for all students. We also introduced a key integration role for school-based district-employed mental health professionals.

Integrating community organizations' personnel and programs into schools is most effective when a structure is in place. Our goal in *School-based Mental Health: A Framework for Intervention* is to present a structure to facilitate the integration of community organizations' personnel and interventions with the school-based mental health (SBMH) services that exist in the school system. Building on the SISSM, we have developed an integrated SBMH framework for school districts in order to ensure they utilize evidence-based interventions that align with their system goals and needs.

Chapter 1 provides a brief summary of *Barriers to Learning*. This includes a classification of barriers to learning and consequences of inadequate intervention. Current education and child and youth mental health reform initiatives are discussed. In addition, the SISSM as a mental health intervention delivery system is introduced.

Chapter 2 introduces a structure for providing integrated school mental health services. This structure, the SISSM Framework, consists of the steps required to integrate community organizations' personnel and interventions into school systems. The SISSM Framework includes governance, funding, accountability, system change protocols, a multi-tiered approach, training guidelines, and the implementation process. Within this SISSM Framework, the chapter highlights the research literature and practice landscape in SBMH integration.

Within the SISSM Framework, chapter 3 provides templates, checklists, and explanations for SBMH governance, funding, accountability, system change protocols, a multi-tiered approach, and training guidelines.

Chapter 4 provides detailed instructions on the SISSM Framework implementation process. Templates for mapping needs and resources as well as planning and evaluating SBMH interventions are provided.

Chapter 5 illustrates how a fictional school district completes the templates from chapters 3 and 4 as it implements the SISSM Framework.

Blank full-page copies of all templates and checklists are provided in the appendices.

A *Review of* Barriers to Learning: The Case for Integrated Mental Health Services in Schools

The book *Barriers to Learning: The Case for Integrated Mental Health Services in Schools* made the case for integrating community-based resources in schools where school-based district-employed mental health professionals play a pivotal role in the process. *School-based Mental Health: A Framework for Intervention* provides the framework necessary to efficiently integrate mental health services in schools. This chapter provides a brief review of *Barriers to Learning.*

It is widely recognized that approximately 20–25 percent of school-age children and youth have diagnosable mental health disorders. However, up to 80 percent of these students do not receive adequate treatment or receive no treatment at all. *Barriers to Learning* categorized common barriers to learning through the lens of what typical school-based mental health (SBMH) support services professionals address in their work. The two major types of barriers to learning categorized are biological-psychological and environmental-circumstantial. However, a combination of the two types of barriers often exists.

The first categorization of barriers to learning, biological-psychological, refers to constitutional or innate predispositions in individual students. These can manifest as psychological or emotional disorders. In *Barriers to Learning,* we divided these barriers into those that are (a) more commonly referred to school-based multi-disciplinary teams and (b) those less commonly referred.

TYPES OF BIOLOGICAL-PSYCHOLOGICAL BARRIERS *MORE COMMONLY* REFERRED FOR SCHOOL INTERVENTION

- Learning disabilities
- Anxiety disorders

- Mood disorders
- Attention and disruptive disorders
- Autism spectrum disorders
- Speech-language disorders
- Intellectual disabilities

TYPES OF BIOLOGICAL-PSYCHOLOGICAL BARRIERS
LESS COMMONLY REFERRED FOR SCHOOL INTERVENTION

- Tic disorders
- Fetal alcohol spectrum disorders
- Eating disorders
- Selective mutism
- Sensory disorders (e.g., vision and hearing)
- Chronic/life-threatening illnesses

The second categorization of barriers to learning is environmental-circumstantial and is based on students' environments, current contexts, and particular circumstances.

ENVIRONMENTAL-CIRCUMSTANTIAL BARRIERS
COMMONLY REFERRED FOR SCHOOL INTERVENTION

- Children/youth exposed to domestic violence
- Child abuse
- Change in family constitution
- Social discrimination
- Economic challenges
- Loss of job/unemployment
- Exposure to mass media

The negative influence of mass media is well documented. Negative media messages and the amount of "screen time" that students are exposed to has increased exponentially recently with more easily accessible personal technology. Recent studies have shown that students spend an average of 6.5 hours a day connected with media. By the age of eighteen, these students will have watched 16,000 simulated murders on television alone.

When barriers to learning in either category are not addressed, or are addressed inadequately, individual and class learning are compromised along with teaching effectiveness. Negative outcomes from inadequate intervention include those listed below:

- Bullying
- School refusal
- Drop-outs
- Addictions (e.g., substance abuse, gambling, and gaming)
- Suicide (ideation, attempts, and completions)
- Youth violence
- Multi-ripple effect

The multi-ripple effect is a hypothetical negative impact on learning and teaching arising from the behavior of students whose barriers to learning have not been adequately addressed. Although the multi-ripple effect is hypothetical, teachers do recognize the occurrence of inappropriate behaviors in students *not originally* facing barriers to learning.

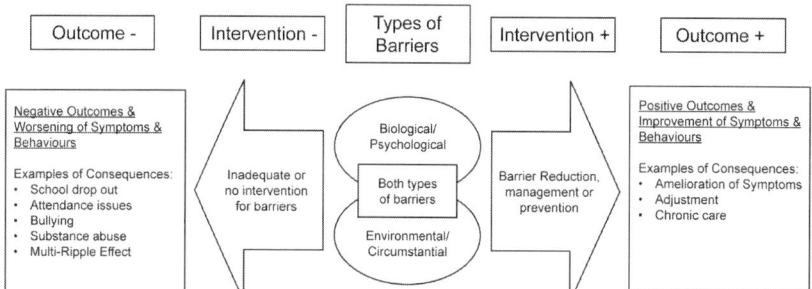

Figure 1.1. Types of Barriers to Learning, Interventions, and Outcomes for Students

Figure 1.1 illustrates a model of intervention outcomes from both adequate and inadequate interventions for barriers to learning.

Prevalence rates were discussed to show that there are a substantial number of students facing a variety of barriers to learning to cumulatively impact both learning and teaching in the classroom. Adding in the fact that up to 80 percent of these students receive inadequate or no intervention at all makes the problem more severe and makes the call for proper intervention more urgent.

RECENT REFORMS IN EDUCATION AND CHILD AND YOUTH MENTAL HEALTH

In *Barriers to Learning*, we discussed key difficulties with current education system reforms. A significant number of these reforms aim to close the achievement gap primarily through improved leadership, accountability, and pedagogy. In our opinion, this approach falls short of addressing many student needs. Although education reformers acknowledge mental health problems in students, they often suggest that mental health interventions be carried out by community services in or out of schools. Community institutions can play a significant role in school mental health intervention; however, without a structure, a plan, or a practical framework to facilitate integration of mental health services into the school system, these goals will not be achieved.

Many current child and youth mental health reform plans include schools. However, the plans as introduced are limited in context and narrow in focus. Current reforms suggest that teachers take on two additional roles: (1) early identifiers of student mental health problems and (2) providers of mental health promotion and prevention. It is our opinion that teachers do not need responsibilities that fall within the realm of mental health intervention, especially when trained mental health professionals can more effectively assume these responsibilities. To date, such reforms have often overlooked the key role that school-based district-employed support services personnel have played and can play in addressing mental health problems in students.

Figure 1.2 provides a graphic representation of common attempts at integration when community institutions provide services in schools without a structural framework that incorporates a role for existing school-based district/board-employed support services. The result is fragmented, and all barriers to learning are not met, as illustrated by the scattered ovals and white spaces in the Venn diagram.

The current practice of simply placing mental health professionals from community institutions into schools to service students has its limitations. Merely collocating community-based mental health professionals in school buildings without understanding the complexity of the educational system and planned integration of services within the system is problematic.

Research has shown that mental health intervention runs more efficiently and effectively when SBMH professionals employed by the board or district provide the services themselves, or at least have a role in the coordination and integration of community services and programs.

When integrating community-based services into schools, school-based support services mental health professionals can be instrumental in providing a seamless delivery of services to ensure the best outcomes for students facing barriers to learning. In order to facilitate this integration process, we developed the School-based Integrated Support Services Model (SISSM).

Figure 1.3 illustrates how SISSM integrates community institutions' personnel into school systems through a core group of school-based support

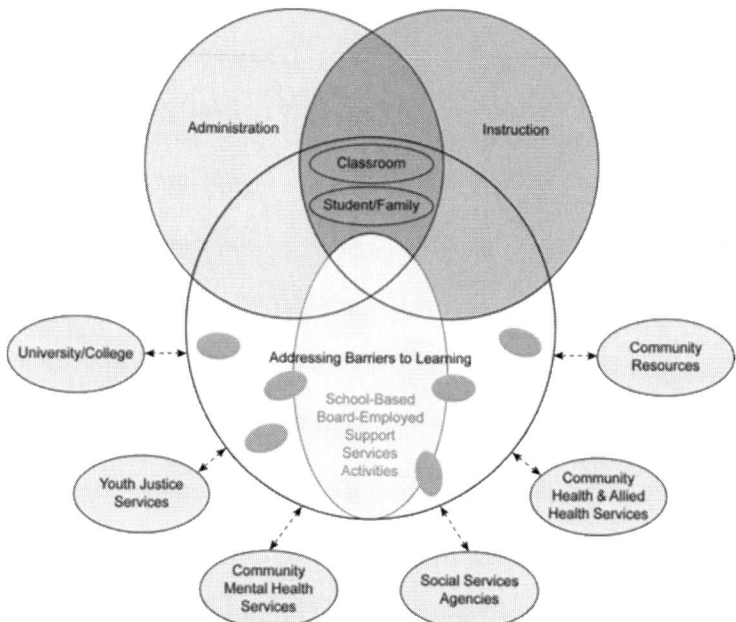

Figure 1.2. *School System Approach to Address Barriers to Learning: School-based Student Support Services Teams and Community Organizations*

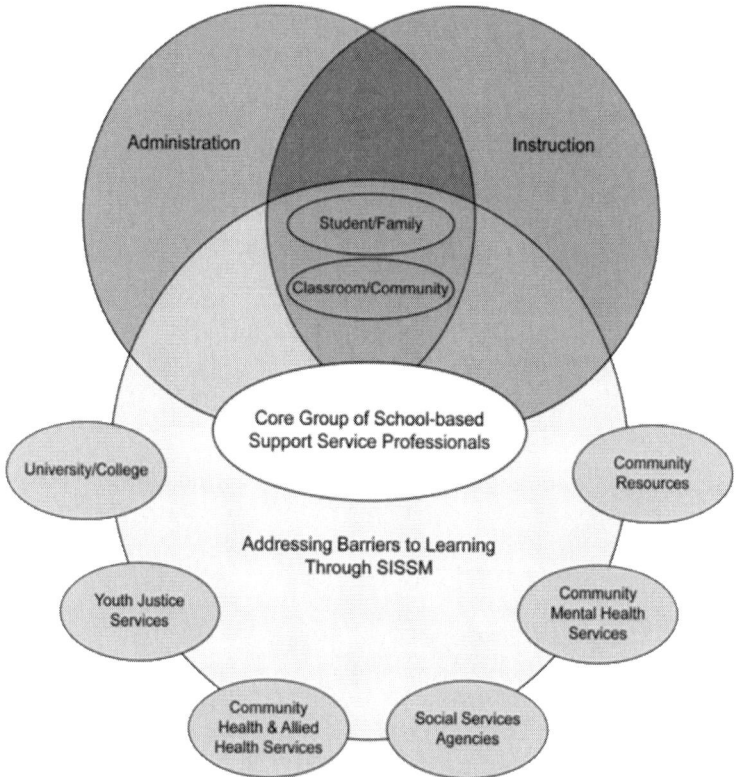

Figure 1.3. *School System Approach to Address Barriers to Learning: SISSM*

services professionals. As stated in *Barriers to Learning*, the core group consists of school-based district-employed support services professionals. In our opinion, these professionals must play a key role in any integration of services into the school system because of their expertise in both the education and mental health areas. We suggested that there be at least one of these professionals assigned to individual schools.

Figure 1.4 provides a flow chart that illustrates the steps required to implement SISSM. We advocate for a mixed top-down/bottom-up approach. In Level 1, child and youth-serving governing bodies (i.e., government departments such as education and child services) mandate the implementation of SISSM. We believe that mandating SISSM (the top-down portion of the approach) is required to implement a population-based approach to addressing barriers to learning.

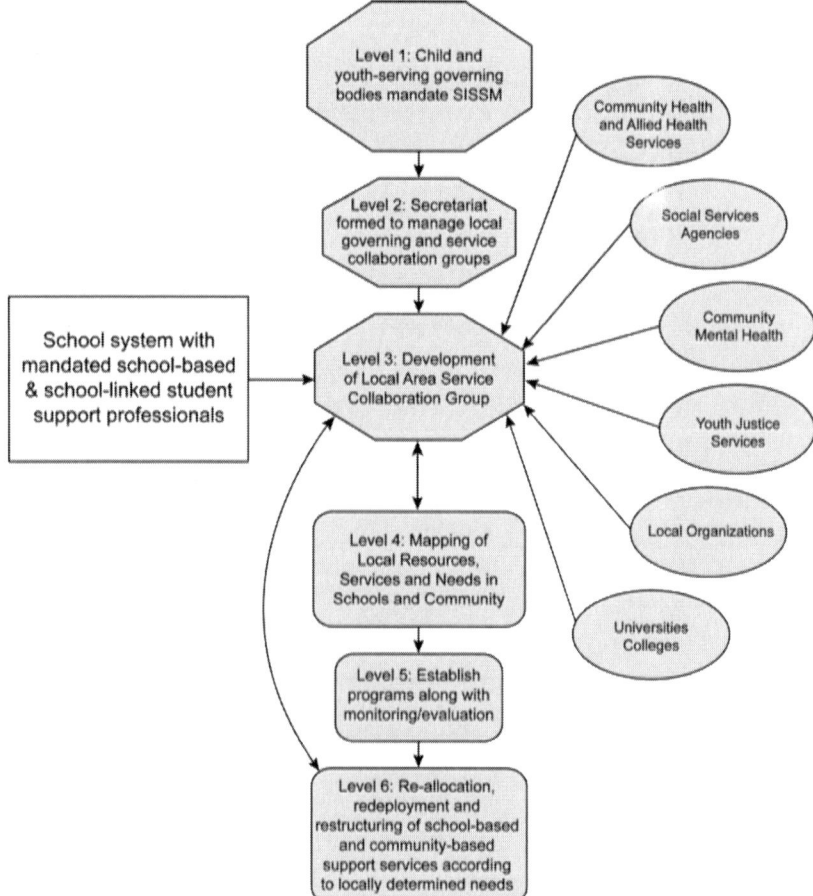

Figure 1.4. *Proposed Implementation of SISSM*

Level 2 denotes the development of an upper level of governance or overarching body. This would be a secretariat with dedicated staff whose responsibility it is to manage the remaining levels of the model's implementation, as well as manage any required preliminary funding to support changes in system delivery. At this level, system-wide guidance and leadership create the readiness for the systematic change to implement SISSM. This entity will ensure the coordination and integration of services with instructional and educational leadership components.

Level 3 comprises the development of multiple service collaboration groups that are locally based. These groups would consist of leaders from both the school system on the left side (educators, administrators, and school-based student support services) and the community organizations depicted on the right side of figure 1.4. Parent and youth representatives also are included in the process. Education and multi-disciplinary professional associations and unions, where they exist, should be involved.

We recommend that the chairperson of each service collaboration group be a school-based district-employed student support professional who already has a managerial role. It is important that the chairperson has a working knowledge of both schools and community organizations. This local group will meet regularly but may rotate meeting locations to different schools and community organization premises to promote a better understanding of each other's cultures, norms, and practices.

In Level 4, the service collaboration group performs a comprehensive mapping activity. This activity consists of enumerating existing local resources, services, and programs, performing a gap analysis, surveying unmet needs, and identifying desired outcomes. Here is where nonproductive services, duplication of services, and fragmentation will be identified. Existing programs need to be catalogued as to which tier of intervention they represent. At the beginning of the process, it is likely that waiting lists for individual services can be addressed, because the primary focus will be indicated/intense individual services—that is, Tier 3.

Resources that can be used to accomplish the tasks in Level 4 were presented, including the Center for Mental Health in Schools at UCLA (smhp .psych.ucla.edu). It is important to map systems for promoting mental health development, prevention, and early intervention of emerging problems, as well as addressing existing chronic and severe problems. By planning for all levels of the continuum of services, *all* tiers of a population-based approach can be addressed.

Level 5 establishes appropriate population-based programs at all tiers according to what was determined by the mapping activity in Level 4. Prioritization of services and tiers is necessary, especially when there are competing needs. Level 5 also establishes monitoring/evaluation structures that are accountable to the service collaboration group, who in turn is accountable to the secretariat.

Level 6 is the reallocation, redeployment, and restructuring of school-based and community-based services according to what has been determined by the previous levels' activities. We realize that needs and resources are not static, so we have included a feedback loop to Level 3, the service collaboration group, as needs and resources change.

ADVANTAGES OF IMPLEMENTING A POPULATION-BASED APPROACH TO BARRIERS TO LEARNING

The structure of SISSM allows schools to more easily utilize a population-based three-tier approach to providing mental health services in schools.

Figure 1.5 shows how support services can provide three tiers of mental health supports in schools.

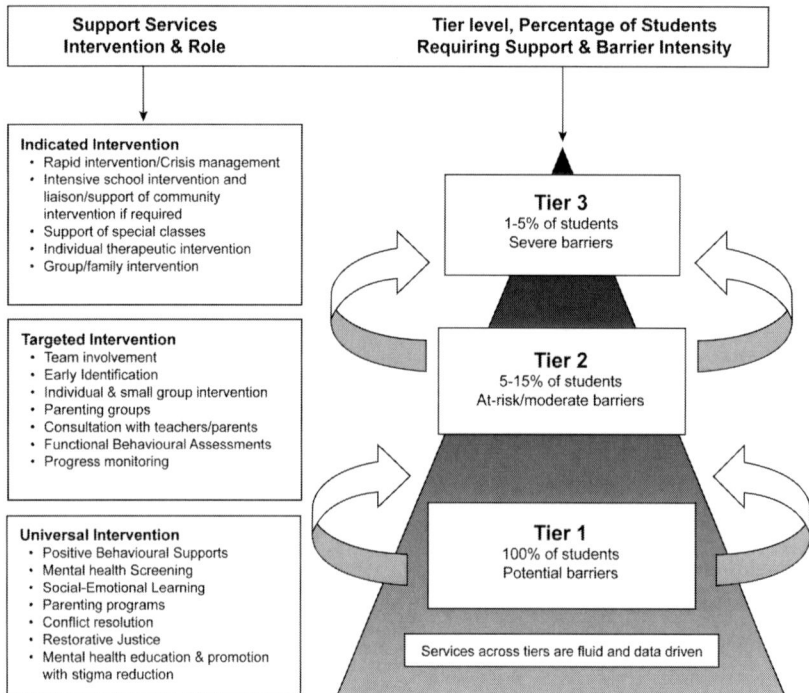

Figure 1.5. *School-based Support Services Interventions and Roles in a Population-based Model*

School-based student support services professionals have knowledge of both education and mental health and thus can play a pivotal role in integrating community-based services into schools. This structure facilitates implementation of population-based supports for both mental health and academic supports, as there is a strong relationship between the two.

Successful integration of community institutions into schools requires the following: (1) a true commitment and ongoing support from all stakeholders, (2) a contingent of school-based, district/board-employed multi-disciplinary mental health professionals, and (3) a structure or framework to facilitate implementation. *School-based Mental Health: A Framework for Intervention* offers a specific and practical framework to integrate SBMH and community-based mental health services.

CHAPTER 2

Current Landscape in SBMH Practices within the SISSM Framework

This chapter presents a detailed portrayal of the current landscape of SBMH practice divided into the sections that comprise the SISSM Framework. The SISSM Framework for SBMH intervention is designed to provide a framework whereby mental health services can be successfully integrated into schools. Inherent within this framework is the flexibility to accommodate the fluidity of the education system. Figure 2.1 presents the SISSM Framework for SBMH intervention.

SISSM Framework for SBMH Intervention						
Governance	Funding	Accountability	System Change Protocols	Multi-tiered Approach	Training	Implementation Process

Figure 2.1. *SISSM Framework for Implementation of SBMH Intervention*

SISSM Framework for SBMH Intervention						
Governance	Funding	Accountability	System Change Protocols	Multi-tiered Approach	Training	Implementation Process

GOVERNANCE

Governance is the key component in the implementation process of SBMH services. Although many new programs in SBMH start at the grassroots level, it is essential that a higher-level entity exists. This entity's responsibilities include providing effective management, direction, and official recognition of the process, as well as providing opportunities for SBMH to expand where required. We have divided the current SBMH governance landscape into three areas: (1) child-serving government departments joint committees, (2) state/provincial/regional SBMH governing entities, and (3) school district–level governance groups.

Child-serving Government Departments Joint Committees

Many state/provincial/regional governments have established an integrated governing structure from key departments responsible for servicing the needs of children and youth. In some jurisdictions, these structures consist of elected and appointed department leaders (e.g., a minister); in other jurisdictions, they consist of high-level nonelected leaders of government departments. One of the provisions of these cross-departmental cabinet-type entities is that they pool funds from different departments or ministries to fund services for children and youth.

There are many cross-government department entities that serve the needs of children and youth. Two examples are discussed below. In the United States in 2009, 22 states legislated and established children's cabinets. These cabinets often develop strategic plans for interagency collaboration through stakeholder involvement, including families and youth (Famularo, 2009).

The state of Massachusetts developed a child cabinet in 2008 entitled the Governor's Child and Youth Readiness Cabinet. Its members include the secretaries for the following departments (the first two are the chairs of the child cabinet):

- Education
- Health and Education
- Administration and Finance
- Housing and Economic Development
- Labor and Workforce Development
- Public Safety and Security
- Child Advocate

The cabinet's purpose is to coordinate and foster efforts to advance collaboration across state departments and agencies.

The District of Columbia formed the Interagency Collaboration and Services Integration Commission in 2007 through the District of Columbia Public Education Reform Amendment Act. School mental health was an integral part of the act. A portion of the legislation speaks to mental health, highlighting the importance of school-based professionals in coordinating integrated mental health and social services for children and youth (Price & Lear, 2008).

The Canadian province of Manitoba developed a similar entity called "Healthy Child Manitoba" in 2007. A Healthy Child Committee of the cabinet was developed and consists of programs, policies, and services that have an impact on the lives of children (Government of Manitoba, 2012). This is a joint departmental partnership from the following government ministries:

- Aboriginal and Northern Affairs
- Children and Youth Opportunities
- Culture, Heritage, and Tourism
- Education
- Family Services
- Labor/Status of Women
- Health
- Healthy Living/Seniors and Consumer Affairs
- Housing and Community Development
- Immigration and Multiculturalism
- Justice

The representatives from these ministries are legislated to meet five times a year, and there is an advisory committee of twelve that represent the demographic and geographic diversity of the province. Half of the committee members must have expertise in prevention, early intervention strategies, child development, or research and evaluation methods. These individuals are drawn from recommendations of parent-child coalitions in the province.

In the United Kingdom, the National Service Framework for Children, Young People, and Maternity Services is in the midst of a ten-year strategy with the goal of setting national standards for children's health and social care. This is facilitated by the establishment of children's trusts, in which departments of Health, Education, and Social Care provide leadership and commission services. For example, in Wales, the three departments mentioned above also include Economic Development and Transport; Culture, Language, and Sport; Environment, Planning, and Countryside; Finance, Local Government, and Public Services; and Social Justice and Regeneration (Welsh Government, 2012).

Child- and youth-based mental health policies can be developed more effectively through collaborative processes taken on by structures such as these "child cabinets." In this way, government policy, programs, and services are integrated. One of the many functions of this group involves providing mental health services for children and youth, and part of this service often includes SBMH (Famularo, 2009).

Even though these types of higher-level government committees consist of ministers or state directors, Famularo (2009) said that in their work, it is important to include input from the public. She suggests these entities regularly convene town hall meetings, focus groups, committees, and task forces and develop and maintain interagency working groups. These working groups must include representatives from all stakeholder groups, especially family and youth, in order to incorporate local needs and represent diversity.

Famularo (2009) states that children's cabinets' roles vary but generally include the following:

- Establish goals and success indicators from strategic plans for member agencies to achieve.
- Provide technical assistance and governance to local jurisdictions, such as distributing funds through grants.
- Develop policy and recommend funding systems to the state governor, such as pooling funds.

This level of governance can be responsible for legislation supporting and mandating population-based SBMH. Any legislation to integrate government departments will also make it easier to integrate data collection and reporting systems between the departments/ministries involved (Ringeisen, Henderson, & Hoagwood, 2003).

State/Provincial/Regional SBMH Governance Entities

Many states, provinces, and regions have legislated and established entities that facilitate the integration of mental health services for children and youth. These entities' responsibilities include (1) facilitating collaboration between schools and child-serving government agencies; (2) overseeing integrated services at the state, provincial, or regional level; and (3) providing the necessary support to the local level, such as districts and schools.

Ringeisen et al. (2003) presented these government entities with additional roles, which include the following:

- Identify where students requiring intervention are located through data-monitoring systems.
- Determine (and ensure) that the resources are available to meet the student needs for intervention.
- Monitor outcomes of SBMH intervention.
- Monitor how SBMH interventions improve academic functioning.
- Monitor how SBMH intervention aligns with school district strategic plans.

The general functions of such types of government entities that are discussed in the SBMH literature can be grouped under the following six categories:

1. Provide and manage necessary funding.
2. Build and support readiness for change.
3. Provide and support training for SBMH service providers.
4. Manage implementation of integrated SBMH services.
5. Provide and support data analysis for implementation of SBMH services.
6. Provide knowledge exchange, translation, and mobilization, which is integral to all the categories above.

School District–Level Governance Groups

Many school districts have developed an additional level of SBMH governance. There are many structural variations at this governance level; however, the state/provincial/regional governance body often dictates the structure of these groups. These school district–level groups direct local district governance and planning activities. Often, a mental health coordinator position is developed and housed at the district level. This role includes the coordination of SBMH activities at the district level as well as overseeing any governance groups that may be at the local level.

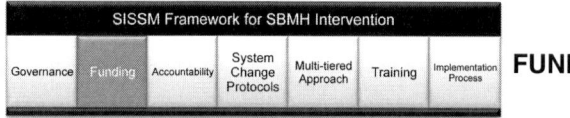 **FUNDING**

In many jurisdictions, it is acknowledged that there are major concerns regarding the distribution of funds and service delivery for child and youth mental health. Recently, the Rand Organization (Sturm, Ringel, Stein, & Kapur, 2011) examined the overall financial picture for mental health services for children and youth in the United States. One key finding is that policymakers were making child and youth mental health funding decisions based on old incidence data. Furthermore, it was suggested that these policymakers had no clear picture of how much was being spent on these services or how many children and youth were actually receiving these mental health services. Additional findings included those listed below:

- About $12 billion annually is being spent on child and youth health care; this is significantly more than previous estimates.
- Most of the money is spent on outpatient care (as opposed to inpatient care); it is believed that a large part of this is *school-based* (this term is not clearly defined).

- About 9 percent of children and youth require mental health care.
- Almost 75 percent of children and youth with mental health problems do not receive proper care.
- Only 5–7 percent are treated by mental health specialists (although this term is not clearly defined); most are seen by their primary care physicians.
- Visible minorities are most likely to not receive mental health care.
- More than $1 billion annually was spent on psychotropic medications, mostly for attention disorders for children under eleven and mostly antidepressants for adolescents.
- Medicaid-covered treatment accounted for only one-quarter of the costs.
- Even when children and youth had private coverage, many of the services were not paid for in this manner.

The Rand report does not reflect an isolated practice. Similar concerns about child and youth mental health spending have been raised in other jurisdictions. In Canada, a 2009 national report found that many of the countries' ten provinces did not have a clear child-and-youth mental health strategy (Canadian Paediatric Society, 2009). Also, small increases in funding for children's mental health were so far behind the inflation rate that there was actually a significant loss in treatment capacity (Office of the Provincial Auditor, 2008).

Currently, there are different methods of funding SBMH interventions. The methods utilized often depend on jurisdiction and how health services, particularly mental health services, are funded. In the United States, sources for funding SBMH interventions include the following:

- School-based government funding
  - Individuals with Disabilities Education Act (IDEA) funds for students who have an Individual Education Plan for emotional issues where mental health services are mandated
  - Safe and Drug-Free Schools and Communities Act
  - General school budgets for high-needs students as an alternative to funding residential- or day-treatment services
  - Internal school support services staff budgets (e.g., psychologists, social workers, counselors)
- Grants
  - Private foundations
  - Public foundations
    - Federal
    - State
    - Local

- Reimbursement programs
  - Medicaid for schools or clinics
  - Private insurance from students' families

This mix of funding sources often makes it difficult to provide sustained and uninterrupted services (e.g., having to wait until the next budget year).

Other jurisdictions—for example, Canada—primarily provide government-based funding for mental health services. In the case of SBMH services, again, governments fund the bulk of services, which may be a joint collaboration between education departments, health, and social services. There may be limited public or private grant funding available to education to provide mental health services in schools. Some families may utilize personal insurance coverage from their employer to provide mental health services for their children. Others may be able to afford private mental health services paid for out of pocket.

Different methods of combining funds for SBMH services have been reported in the literature, such as "braided" or "blended" funding. This type of funding refers to utilizing more than one source of funds to provide SBMH services. Currently, many urban school districts in the United States utilize blended and braided funding. Schools are not licensed as mental health clinics; therefore, they cannot bill insurance and state funders for these services. Thus, they must enter into a partnership with a licensed agency in order to access funds from these sources.

Blended funding is a combination of school district and outpatient mental health center funding (Lever, Stephan, Axelrod, & Weist, 2004). A braided funding model incorporating funds from a school district, several foundations, a children's hospital, and third-party insurance providers is described in Kilkenny, Katz, and Baron's (2009) work. Some of the reasoning for adopting these funding models includes the following:

- Schools received a percentage of the fee-for-service billings
- The new system added a link with a university mental health service, which provided access to
  - other mental health centers
  - psychiatric fellows
  - the emergency room
  - specialty clinics
- Better continuity of care for students

However, both groups of authors raise several concerns with this funding system, which include the following:

- Additional expenses
  - part of a salary for a program director
  - clerical staff to prepare the paperwork to process billing and manage the income received from the third-party payers (e.g., insurance companies)
- SBMH clinic mental health staff had to learn how to track services for the billing, which cut into time allotted for their clinical services
- Difficult to fund prevention and early intervention services
- Fee-for-service funding tends to be feasible only for students with diagnosable mental health disorders (billable hours quotas) that are generally Tier 3 intense services
- Clinicians are not connected with the school and rarely interact with any school personnel, particularly school-based mental staff (e.g., school psychologists, school social workers)
- Fee-for-service interventions cannot be provided for students who do not have insurance or whose parents are not willing to sign on to the new braided or blended funding system
- Confidentiality issues for parents and students
- Presence of psychiatry brings on issues about medication and diagnoses that parents and students may not accept
- Students may have been able to access SBMH services previously without as much family involvement as that required by agencies

Although SBMH funding can come from many sources, how it is spent is not always well scrutinized. Concerns have been raised that these funds do not always reach direct frontline services. For example, in some areas, a high proportion of funds are spent on directors and coordinators as opposed to frontline services delivered by highly trained and credentialized personnel.

In summary, there are many different methods of providing funds for expanding SBMH services. Grant-based funding is commonly utilized, but it is most often based on a complex application and reporting process. This process takes professionals' time and resources away from direct services because of the time required to apply for and report on the grants. Some school boards may elect to purchase the services of professional grant writers; however, this practice takes away needed funds from direct services as well. In addition, grant-based funding practice often hinders long-range program planning as well as employment and thus staffing stability.

SISSM Framework for SBMH Intervention						
Governance	Funding	Accountability	System Change Protocols	Multi-tiered Approach	Training	Implementation Process

ACCOUNTABILITY

Current global economic concerns are affecting fiscal resources, which often results in downsizing public services. Within this trend is the movement toward privatizing services, contracting out, and a customer/client orientation that demands quality standards with performance measures and benchmarks (Thompson, 1999). In addition, there is a government movement toward mandating integration of publicly funded services. In the case of child and youth mental health, the common plan is to integrate community-based mental health services into schools. As a result of these trends, accountability will be playing a more significant role in the delivery of mental health services.

The mental health literature—and health literature in general—has an abundance of material available for mental health providers to specifically improve accountability systems. Initially, accountability merely referred to fiscal responsibility. Recent additions include (1) product or output measures (e.g., number of clients seen, number of sessions and waiting lists), (2) adherence to standards of practice, (3) staff qualification and performance levels, and (4) following budget limitations. Recently, accountability systems have become more complex to include specific outcome measures that are tied to the organizations' strategic directions and goals. This type of accountability is referred to as performance accountability (Thomspon, 1999).

Performance accountability measures more than output (i.e., beyond measuring how many students were seen). Performance accountability measures policy outcomes, and as such is directly linked with policy goals and objectives. Thusly, both programs and policymakers (service delivery providers and governments) are held accountable. Without this level of accountability, programs can be determined to be effective, but they are not reflecting movement according to the organization's and/or government's policies. Therefore, the data that are collected do not reflect policy directives. For example, headcounts of students seen by support services professionals are not useful unless the goal is to serve as many students and parents as possible. Considerable human and financial resources are spent gathering large amounts of such data. If the school district's goal is to improve student achievement and well-being, this accountability system is of little overall benefit.

One performance accountability system often used in the human services area is Results-Based Accountability (RBA). Accountability indicators are determined by working backward from wanted results and then are used to determine the means to get there. RBA is often used when strategic directions are being planned. Other systems include variations of quality improvement, or continuous quality improvement, in which information is gathered in order to determine the progress of specific programs and adjust as necessary to ensure improvements.

Comprehensive information on accountability for mental health services is discussed by Thompson (1999) and McEwan and Goldner (2001). Their suggestions for developing accountability include measures that

- are achievable (not overly complex);
- utilize available data and information systems wherever possible;
- ensure the measures represent client, stakeholder, and funder and meet their expectations (involve them in development of measures);
- are chosen strategically—some should demonstrate link to productivity, some should measure performance;
- are conceptually clear and understandable—desired direction of movement is clear (positive or negative);
- are linked clearly and integrated with goals of the organization;
- are operationally defined;
- have measurable validity and reliability;
- allow comparisons when required;
- provide a common vision (e.g., better outcomes for children);
- are shared widely;
- acknowledge poor performance and include commitment for corrective action; and
- are regularly reported.

The authors caution that it is important to keep expectations of improvement realistic. In addition, it is important to use caution when interpreting short-term results, as they may not be accurate and sensitive enough to show change. It is suggested that setting up an accountability system includes planning for sufficient timelines to demonstrate positive impacts on program change. Measuring results also requires time, money, and personnel trained in evaluation. They suggest that when implementing new programs, necessary funding is set aside to cover the costs for developing outcome measures required for accountability.

There are several types of accountability measures. Thompson (1999) listed many, including the following:

- Financial
  - Cost per client served
  - Resources allocated
- Program outputs
  - Number of sessions
  - Number of assessments
- Program standards
  - Staff-client ratios
  - Spaces per 1,000 population
- Client characteristics (demographics)
  - Age
  - Sex
  - Poverty status
  - Learning readiness
- Program outcomes (positive measures—increase in, and negative measures—reduction in)
  - Improvement in well-being
  - Symptom reduction
  - Reduction in ER visits
- Client satisfaction
  - With service
  - With staff

School and child and youth mental health systems have widely differing accountability systems; it is not surprising that there is a paucity of information on accountability for SBMH. School systems historically used standards-based accountability systems—namely, performance on large-scale standardized tests. However, more recently, many school systems have been mandated to develop strategic plans with measurable goals and objectives at the state/provincial/regional district and school level.

Governments have recently encouraged, and in some cases mandated, integrated practice partnerships between schools and community mental health providers. The integration of SBMH can include many levels, such as service delivery, administrative support, or development of policies. When these initiatives are mandated, they often come with specific accountability requirements for each practice partner. However, a significant problem with integrating schools and community mental health providers is that they have vastly different accountability systems that are not always easily coordinated. Unless this issue is addressed from the onset of the partnership, the resulting multiple layers of accountability can compromise service delivery and intervention effectiveness. It is important to provide sufficient resources to integrate accountability systems for SBMH intervention.

A unique system of organizational integration was developed by Limbrick in the United Kingdom (Limbrick, 2012). He developed a system called Team Around the Child (TAC) as a formula for private and public organizations to work together creating a significant role for the service user, particularly clients with multifaceted conditions requiring the services of numerous agencies. However, TAC can be used in all areas where multiple agencies work with particular service users.

TAC improves on the more common top-down power structures in vertical child service organizations. Limbrick utilizes a novel "horizontal" organizational structure in which decisions and accountability are shared between empowered service users and skilled leadership. A new role is given for practitioners as "keyworkers," who are lead professionals who integrate services for specific children. Horizontal teamwork is supported where working practices are more efficient and consist of all agencies providing interdependent services.

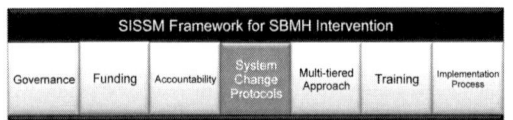

SYSTEM CHANGE PROTOCOLS

It is vitally important to address system change issues when implementing SBMH interventions. There is an entire literature devoted to system change in education, specifically developed for introducing curricular innovation. This system change is generally designed to increase and sustain academic achievement (e.g., Fullan, 2010).

Implementing SBMH programs requires change at many levels, especially for educators and mental health professionals. SBMH practitioners must be trained in system change methods required to adopt, implement, and sustain effective interventions for students (Kratochwill, Volpiansky, Clements, & Ball, 2007). Research in implementation science has resulted in the development of methods for "scaling up." Scaling up refers to ensuring effective implementation of changes in practice, programs, and interventions for the entire system—in this case, schools (Fixsen, Naoon, Blasé, Friedman, & Wallace, 2005).

Change theory states that when all innovation starts at the same point, widely different outcomes are achieved. Rowling (2007) suggests that introducing mental health change in schools should utilize the change theory concept of multi-finality, in which similar outcomes are reached from different starting points. Schools are at different stages of readiness for mental health reforms and thus require different levels of assistance introducing SBMH interventions. All schools, therefore, should not expect to start at the same place and expect the same outcomes when implementing SBMH practices.

It is expected that certain schools will be resistant to providing integrated SBMH services. Rowling makes recommendations on how to address this challenge: SBMH planners must make a commitment to overcoming expected resistance by working toward achieving legitimacy and status in schools where academics are still the sole focus. This can be achieved by tailoring programs to the needs and goals of school districts, addressing diversity, and always including all stakeholders. Schools have to change from addressing school mental health issues from a reactive perspective to a more balanced approach that enhances school mental health for all students in a preventative and positive manner (Rowling, 2007).

There are numerous systems available for introducing change in schools. All have variations of multiple sequential steps designed to ensure maximum adoption of change. For example, Fixsen et al. (2005) delineated six stages for introducing new programs. These stages are as follows, with explanatory comments adapted from Sugai (2012):

1. Exploration and Adoption: A school district utilizes specific data on student behavior to determine a specific student mental health need. A pilot project is initiated in a few schools. The district implements a mental health prevention program listed on an evidence-based intervention database.
2. Program Installation: The school district provides the necessary staffing and funds as well as training to run the mental health intervention in the selected schools for the pilot project.
3. Initial Implementation: The school district runs and evaluates the program.
4. Full Operation: The pilot project is found to be successful. The school district invests the required resources to expand the intervention throughout the district.
5. Innovation: The school district continually modifies the intervention within the bounds of treatment fidelity in order to meet the school district's needs.
6. Sustainability: The school district plans for and addresses changes in personnel and other educational constructs to ensure sustainability of the intervention.

A change system has been developed from the school psychology perspective, specifically to introduce positive behavior supports in schools (Ervin & Schaughency, 2008). These researchers identified four phases of system change:

1. Creating Readiness is Phase I. This creates an official and psychological climate for change. Specific individuals, often called "change agents," are placed into the system to encourage and facilitate the planned changes. Change agents are required to develop interest and consensus for the planned change in the school and community organizations. This is accomplished by disseminating information about potential benefits and relevance for stakeholders. For example, teachers would be told that the new program would decrease classroom behavior problems.
2. Initial Implementation is Phase II. Here, temporary mechanisms are developed to facilitate the implementation of the new system. A steering committee determines the sequence and strategies needed to begin implementation. It is important to evaluate the process of implementation with ongoing feedback from all stakeholders in order to accommodate minor adjustments. Although significant changes may not occur yet at this point, this is not the time to measure outcomes.
3. Institutionalization is Phase III. As the new system becomes embedded in the school districts' practice, the activities of change agents are gradually reduced until they are no longer required. Promoting the changes, endorsing district ownership of the new system, and planning ongoing capacity building to address fluid school environments (e.g., staff changes) ensure sustainability.
4. Ongoing Evolution is Phase IV. Outcomes are measured and evaluated. Changes in the system structure are now addressed. A knowledge dissemination structure is developed to ensure that any new knowledge (e.g., new SBMH interventions) will be incorporated in the system. It is also important to ensure the staff interest is maintained as "the novelty wears off."

Communication plans are essential when a school system changes to a population-based approach for SBMH. Price and Lear (2008) suggested that such communication plans assist stakeholders in understanding population-based services. In addition, these stakeholders need to be made aware of the progress of the new system. This can be accomplished by (1) sharing information about the new system that is going to be implemented, (2) specifying what interventions are being implemented for the new system, and (3) reviewing what has been implemented. They suggest utilizing newsletters, websites, and social media.

SISSM Framework for SBMH Intervention						
Governance	Funding	Accountability	System Change Protocols	Multi-tiered Approach	Training	Implementation Process

MULTI-TIERED APPROACH

The research and practice literature in SBMH services promotes a multi-tiered approach to services for students. This multi-tiered, or population-based approach, developed from the public health model, utilizes different tiers of intervention depending on the needs of the population (Kutash, Duchnowski, & Lynn, 2006). Rowling (2007) differentiates this approach with the more limiting student-based single issue "medical model."

Sugai, through the Center on Positive Behavior Interventions & Supports in the United States, refers to population-based support as Multi-Tiered Systems of Support (MTSS). MTSS is defined as "a whole school, data driven, prevention-based framework for improving learning outcomes for all students through a layered continuum of evidence-based practices and systems" (Sugai, 2012). Prevention is practiced through two approaches, addressing problem behaviors and promoting pro-social behaviors. Problem behaviors are addressed by (1) preventing existing behaviors from intensifying and becoming more challenging, (2) preventing the development of new problem behaviors, and (3) addressing the conditions that produce or maintain problem behaviors. Promoting pro-social behaviors includes providing the conditions necessary to produce, enhance, and maintain positive behaviors as well as teach them.

Figure 2.2 illustrates a modification to the commonly utilized three-part triangle representation of multi-tiered supports, specifically for student mental health. Weist and his colleagues add a fourth tier at the bottom of the triangle, under the universal tier. This tier includes interventions to promote positive school environments and enhancement of relationships within schools (Weist, Steigler, Stephan, Cox, & Vaughan, 2009).

In MTSS, all students receive universal supports, and subsets of these students receive targeted and intense supports. Universal services are for all students and generally include mental health promotion as well as programs designed to prevent the development of mental health problems, such as building resiliency. These services are aimed not only at students but also need to include all staff in the school and all students' families, and they should be delivered in all school settings as well (Sugai, 2012). Targeted services provide early intervention services for subsets of students deemed to be at risk for mental health problems. Indicated or intense services are for the smaller subsets of students requiring high levels of intervention for moderate-to-severe mental health problems.

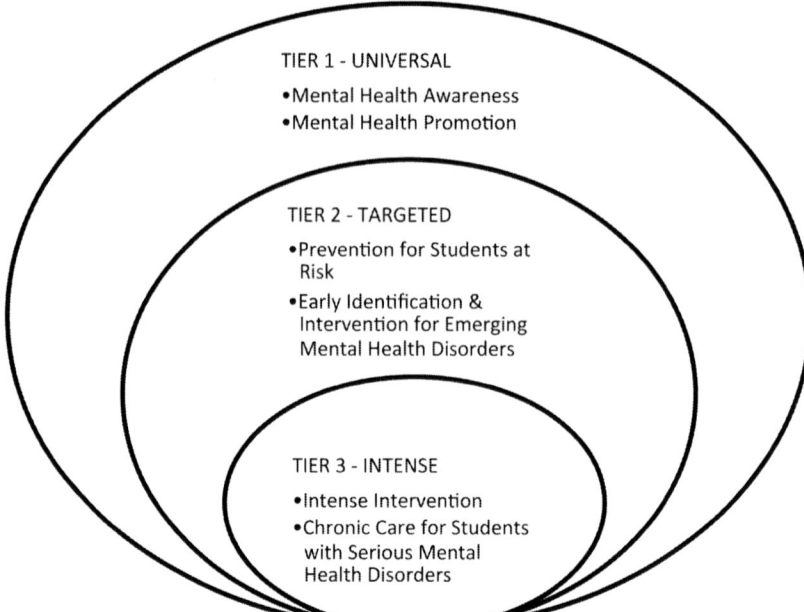

Figure 2.2. *Population-based Tiers for School Mental Health*

Different students therefore receive different levels, or "dosages," of intervention. Simply providing SBMH interventions is not sufficient; it is important to determine, within an MTSS approach, who are the subjects of the intervention, when is the best time to provide the intervention (e.g., time of school year), and what is the goal of the intervention. Although the approach is essentially temporal in nature, students may enter at the targeted or intense level when required (Ervin & Schaughency, 2008).

Within the MTSS approach, not every school has to provide interventions at every tier. In addition, individual students should not be deemed to be at only one tier. There has been considerable discussion about the propensity to call students exhibiting severe behaviors Tier 3 students.

In an effort to avoid this problem, Sugai (2012) developed a system of labeling the intervention, as opposed to the student, depending on the specific need determined by data gathering. Students experiencing behavior and/or academic difficulties are not going to require services at the same level for each of their areas of academic and behavioral need. Just as students do not require the same intensity of academic supports for every subject, students with behavioral or mental health difficulties do not require the same level of intervention for each area of behavioral functioning. For example, data collected on one student determined that he requires individual Tier 3 intervention for his difficulty paying attention in class. Data collected on the whole class determined that he required Tier 2 intervention in a small group for developing more appropriate social skills. Data collected in the school determined that he would participate in a whole-school Tier 1 intervention for bullying prevention.

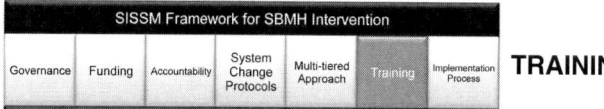

TRAINING

Specific training for SBMH providers in the ability to provide "flexibility within fidelity" is crucial. Without this training, intervention efficacy cannot be assured. There are specific problems in the transportability of evidence-based practices (EBPs) into schools. Reinke, Herman, Stormont, Brooks, and Darney (2010) discussed such problems including the difficulty of implementing these interventions with fidelity within the complexity and fluidity of school environments. Schools do not have the carefully controlled conditions that exist in lab-based randomized controlled studies. Even within the lab, there are many variations in individual client needs that require clinical decisions for implementation of manualized interventions. Thus, the concept of "flexibility within fidelity" was coined by Kendall and his team (Kendall, Gosch, Furr, & Sood, 2008) to refer to the clinical variations to address client variations within the framework of the treatment manual. This requirement extends even further for the provision of mental health intervention in the school setting, such as addressing time available for sessions.

In the SBMH literature, training is often divided into two areas: The first area is "preservice" training, which refers to professional training programs such as graduate programs for psychologists, social workers, and teachers. The second area is "postservice" training, which refers to training provided to individuals already employed in their field, including school mental health professionals, classroom teachers, special education teachers, consultants, administrators, and policymakers.

Preservice Training

Training for mental health practitioners to be employed as school-based support services personnel is generally discipline specific. However, there are documents published by various discipline-related organizations that provide guidelines for training school-based service competencies. For example, the

National Association of School Psychologists (NASP) publishes the Blueprint for Training and Practice (NASP, 2006). Many of NASP's nine recommended competency domains would be appropriate to train all disciplines providing integrated SBMH services. These competencies include the following:

- Interpersonal and collaborative skills
- Diversity awareness and sensitive service delivery
- Technological applications (respecting legislation, confidentiality, and privacy)
- Professional, legal, ethical, and social responsibility
- Data-based decision-making
- System-based service delivery
- Enhancing wellness, social skills, mental health, and life competencies

Regardless of recommended competencies, these recommendations do not always translate into practice. For example, a review of the syllabi for mental health practitioner graduate training found that normally recommended competencies were not present (Gelzheiser, 2009; Berzin & O'Connor, 2010). Furthermore, current SBMH practitioners lacked some competencies, particularly in system-based service delivery (Nastasi, Hatzichristou, Jones, Schanding, & Yetter, 2010). One possible solution to the problems with competencies in SBMH is a multi-university internship program that developed accountability standards for school psychology internship level training in system-wide approaches such as positive behavior supports (Morrison, Graden, & Barnett, 2009).

Some educator training programs are incorporating instruction in mental health awareness. It is important to differentiate this instruction from training for mental health clinicians. This instruction can include differentiating behavior problems and mental health disorders, as well as methods for promoting good mental health and build resilience in students.

Postservice Training

Working with a population-based approach may be new for many SBMH professionals. It can be challenging for personnel used to practicing clinical casework to begin universal mental health promotion and prevention work. Adding mental health promotion, prevention, and early intervention services will move some clinicians out of what Domitrovich, Bradshaw, Greenberg, Embry, Poduska, and Ialongo (2009) call their "expert role" comfort zone into one that may require more collaboration with school and outside agency staff.

Activities that are not seen as clinical or are not based on diagnoses may also be undervalued and not challenging to some clinicians.

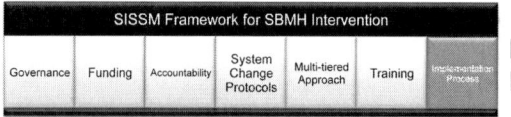

IMPLEMENTATION PROCESS

Implementing SBMH services is a complex process that requires careful planning at the district, school, and classroom level. Many process guides are available to assist in the implementation of integrated SBMH services.

Building and Maintaining Partnerships

SBMH practice inherently involves collaboration and partnerships with a variety of organizations, as described in chapter 1. The organizations are categorized as community mental health services, community health and allied health services, social service agencies, youth justice services, community resources, and universities and colleges.

Building and maintaining SBMH partnerships, according to the SBMH literature, requires the support of key leaders at the school board level. However, this can be problematic when leaders are focused on strict academic accountability systems (e.g., high-stakes testing) in which academic instruction has and may continue to override any mental health programming. In order to begin addressing such a challenge, it is often necessary to increase the entire school community's (including parents') understanding of the relationship between mental health and academic achievement (Cummings & Doll, 2008).

When developing partnerships, the SBMH literature recommends that it is important to build collaborative relationships and identify benefits and expectations from both sides. This will facilitate drawing up a contract (e.g., a memorandum of agreement) to address cost sharing, administration, clinical work, and revenue allocation, as well as provide a forum to voice concerns from both sides—at the upper management and the clinician level (Lever et al., 2004).

Partnerships can leave both school-based and community-based professionals concerned about job security as well as their students' or patients' eligibility for services. There may also be concerns about increased paperwork and regulations affecting current practice in terms of autonomy and creativity in choosing interventions (Lever et al., 2004).

The literature in SBMH suggests that a leadership group be formed within the school district (or school) that crosses all disciplines. These groups usually have links to the community resources that will be asked to integrate into the SBMH programs. Researchers in this area recommend that sufficient time be allocated to build trust, establish clear understandings concerning roles and responsibilities, and develop clear procedures and protocols to link the organizations with the school and/or district to integrate services (Cummings & Doll, 2008).

Supervision in Partnerships

The SBMH literature states that supervision issues can arise when clinicians from community-based settings begin working in schools. Working off-site from their center, these clinicians require a particular type of oversight and supervision. Their agency supervisor and the supervisor of the school-based practitioners need to identify common grounds for supervision of the integrated programs within their own particular supervision practices. These supervisors need to develop an agreement regarding how supervision occurs within the school-based program (Lever et al., 2004).

Supervision issues can also arise with respect to regulations and monitoring of practice. Community-based mental health professionals practice with a different set of regulations and monitoring systems than SBMH professionals. For example, in community-based practice, patients may require a psychiatric diagnosis, documentation, and timelines, and charting procedures must be followed (Lever et al., 2004). School-based professionals may not have to meet these requirements; their documentation may include simply numbers of students served and nature of cases. The school-based professionals may need to alter their reporting activities to comply with stricter regulations from the partnership situation. This may be a fundamental change to the way both community- and school-based personnel and their supervisors practice within the realm of SBMH.

Developing Goals

The SBMH literature states that the goals of intervention must be relevant to all the stakeholders. For schools, reducing mental health symptoms may not be specific enough and too far from academic goals. Examples of goals relevant to schools would be reducing stress on school staff by raising achievement levels and reducing disruptive behaviors in the classroom (Ringeisen et al., 2003). It is also important to align SBMH programs with school goals, particularly school-improvement documentation. This is often required at school and district levels in many jurisdictions (Elias, Zins, Graczyk, & Weissberg, 2003).

Mapping Needs and Resources in SBMH

Many school districts and jurisdictions are mandating the development of a school district mental health strategy. This would be an area in which visions, missions, and broad goals would be developed. Specific strategic directions would be locally based variations of implementing a population-based mental health system in a district.

Most of the literature on SBMH states that mapping student needs is an integral part of SBMH services. Mapping provides the data necessary to make decisions about appropriate intervention. It is important to map both the mental health needs and risk factors of the students in the school and/or district. Baker (2008) suggests administering mental health screening and surveys to students; others suggest examining utilization of local mental health resources and demographic data that are associated with risk factors for mental health problems (Center for Mental Health in Schools at UCLA, 2012a).

Screening

Student mental health screening can be a useful component of a school's mental health strategy when it is used to identify student mental health needs and not considered a diagnostic tool. However, if the screening process is wrongly applied, the results can be easily misinterpreted and misleading. Screening utilizing a multiple-gating screening system is best, as discussed by Weist, Rubin, Moore, Adelsheim, and Wrobel (2007). This system has three major components:

- Gate 1—*first-level screening administration*: Screening tools are administered to the specified group, which can include students, teachers, and parents. Many school districts use commercially available screening tools. Alternately, some school districts construct their own screening tools—for example, having teachers provide lists of students exhibiting concerning behaviors.
- Gate 2—*first-level screening evaluation*: School mental health professionals process and interpret the data from the screening tool(s) and determine which students meet a predetermined cut-off point.
- Gate 3—*second-level screening and evaluation*: Students who meet the predetermined cut-off point are interviewed and/or assessed by school

mental health professionals. This level is designed to identify false positives and determine which students truly have the mental health problems identified by the screening tool.

There are many benefits to screening students for mental health problems. In this process, schools can identify and treat as many students as possible before such problems become severe. Treating these students before their problems become severe can enhance the students' academic success and generate overall benefits for the students' families, teachers, classmates, and even society concerning the students' future productivity. Benefits for the classroom include reducing what Lean and Colucci (2010) refer to as the multi-ripple effect. This term is defined as the hypothetical impact on classmates' academic, emotional, and social functioning from the behavior of students in that classroom whose mental health problems are inadequately addressed.

As mentioned above, the decision to use screeners in an SBMH program requires careful consideration. The Center for Mental Health in Schools at UCLA (2012a) and Weist et al. (2007) discuss key issues regarding SBMH screening that should be considered before the necessary time, cost, and effort are expended. They include the following factors:

- Is the school(s) an appropriate place to screen for mental health?
- Is there a proper informed-consent process for the students and their parents?
- Are privacy rights being protected for both the students and their families?
- Is the screening scheduled at an appropriate time during the school year?
- Which students should be screened, and at what grades?
- What is the validity and reliability of the screener?
- How likely and available is appropriate follow-up to identify screening errors with second-level screening?
- How available is treatment for students who are screened as having mental health issues? (This can be an ethical issue if there is no available treatment.)
- How will the school address potential negative consequences from screening, such as students being stigmatized or false positive cases not followed up properly?

The literature on child and youth mental health indicates that child and adolescent mental health screening tools are not as effective in detecting mental health problems as ones used for adult populations. There is a lower predictive value in screening children and adolescents for mental health disorders, particularly for disorders that are more internalizing, such as anxiety. With respect to screening errors, there are many more false positives screened in children than false negatives (Goodman, Ford, Simmons, Gatward, & Meltzer, 2000; Gould, Greenberg, Velting, & Shaffer, 2003).

One method of addressing some of these disadvantages is to screen positively—that is, to measure resilience and competencies. Examples include the Devereux Student Strengths Assessment (LeBuffe, Shapiro, & Naglieri, 2009) and the Social-Emotional Assets and Resilience Scales (Merrell, 2010). These measures are designed to guide universal and targeted intervention strategies.

Surveys

Many websites are available that include scientifically sound surveys to determine school mental health needs according to the perspectives of students, teachers, and parents. For example, the Mindmatters program from Australia (http://www.mindmatters.edu.au/resources_and_downloads/mindmatters_audits_and_surveys_link.html) provides surveys for all education stakeholders. In the United States, the Collaborative for Academic, Social, and Emotional Learning's website has a section on needs and outcome measures (http://casel.org/in-schools/assessment/needs-and-outcome).

Some jurisdictions, such as Ontario, Canada, have mandated school climate surveys. (See http://www.edu.gov.mb.ca/k12/specedu/fas/pdf/3.pdf for an example.)

Student Risk Factors

The SBMH literature suggests that community mental health utilization data be examined when local needs for SBMH implementation are being determined. Price and Lear (2008) recommend examining data to determine which areas may be underserved in community mental health service. This type of data can provide direction for universal and targeted interventions to reduce risk factors. It is also suggested that several years of data are examined in order to determine trends to inform needs and avoid using data from one year that had unusual results.

Student Competencies/Resilience/Protective Factors

When determining needs, the literature indicates that an often-missed data set includes student competencies and protective factors. As mentioned in the "screening" section above, screening for student competencies and protective factors can identify students who are lacking in this area. Results of such surveys can identify students with limited competencies and inadequate protective factors. Information from these surveys can then identify specific needs that guide the development and implementation of SBMH programs.

A comprehensive list of protective factors for students was developed by Stiegler (2012), which includes the following:

- A positive vision for the school developed by and shared with all stakeholders
- Reasonable ratios of students to teachers and support staff
- Schools that present a safe, welcoming, and positive atmosphere
- Schools that promote and encourage culturally sensitive family involvement
- Appropriate support and professional development for teachers and support staff
- Support and accountability for the diverse needs of students
- A trusting and caring school environment for all stakeholders
- Student pro-social behaviors taught and supported, including problem-solving and coping skills

One well-researched protective factor for students is positive school climate. SBMH practices in a multi-tiered approach, such as positive behavior supports, promote positive school climate, also known as school connectedness. School connectedness occurs when students in a school believe that the adults in the school care about them, particularly for their learning and for them as individuals. Factors associated with a positive school climate have been gathered into numerous checklists, which schools can use to determine SBMH needs.

The Wingspread Declaration on School Connectedness (2004) was developed by a group of educators who identified three major factors that determine school connectedness:

- Support for learning with high academic standards
- Positive student-adult relationships
- Physical and emotional safety

This group of educators also declared that positive school climate promotes motivated and engaged students who have overall better attendance, which increases academic achievement.

The SBMH literature includes many methods to map child and youth mental health resources in the school community. Cummings and Doll (2008) suggest this activity be done not to highlight deficiencies but to determine strengths. These authors summarize the material available from the website of the Center for Mental Health in Schools at UCLA (2012b) that describes resource mapping as a complex activity that includes four basic components:

1. Mapping roles and placements of school and community personnel
2. Mapping all existing mental health programs
3. Mapping financial resources available for facilities, equipment, and personnel
4. Mapping school and community policies that limit or promote the provision of children's mental health services

Resource mapping is a crucial step in the planning and implementation of SBMH services. The literature on SBMH intervention tends to suggest mapping personnel and programs. However, financing and policies are not often sufficiently considered when mapping resources.

Research has demonstrated that the provision of evidence-based services ran more smoothly and had less teacher resistance when practitioners were already employed by the schools, because they were better connected with students and school staff (Massey, Armstrong, Boroughs, Henson, & McCash, 2005; Crisp, Gudmundsen, & Shirk, 2006).

Ratios

Many discussions of school-based support services professionals include ratios. This ratio generally refers to one full-time equivalent position to x number of students.

An international study of school psychologist ratios of fifty-one United Nations countries was conducted in 2007. The mean ratio was 1:1,631. Thirteen countries had ratios of 1:2,000 or lower, including the United States, Canada, Australia, Denmark, Israel, Switzerland, and Turkey (Jimerson, Stewart, Skokut, Cardenas, & Malone, 2012). Recommended ratios are often published by organizations for different school-based support services professionals. The National Association of State Boards of Education (2012) generally does not specify ratios, but those states that do specify them range from 1:1,000 to 1:3,000.

School social workers' ratios also are not often specified, but the ones that are generally reside in the 1:2,500 range, except for one jurisdiction in the

United States where each school is mandated to have one full-time school so-cial worker. Both the National Association of School Psychologists (1:1,000) (Charvat, 2005) and the National Association of Social Workers (1:400) pro-vide recommendations for school-based service ratios (NASW, 2012). NASP recently changed its recommended ratio range to 1:500–1:700 for integrated school psychology practice (NASP, 2010). In Canada, recent studies reveal a wide disparity for school psychologist ratios within and between provinces, ranging from 1:1,000 to 1:10,000 students; however, the recommended ratio is 1:1,000 (Saklofske, Schwean, Bartell, Mureika, Andrews, Derevensky, & Janzen, 2007). Ratios for school counselors are generally specified as 250 students per counselor (Skalski & Smith, 2006).

Two important components of SBMH services are ensuring proper recruit-ment and screening of SBMH staff. Some SBMH policymakers state that staff recruitment and screening are often more important than the selection of evidence-based programs. Specific characteristics of SBMH personnel, such as their clinical orientation, should be coordinated with specific inter-ventions. This approach may avoid implementation problems, burnout and high-practitioner turnover as well as increase effectiveness of the intervention (Price & Lear, 2008).

GAP ANALYSIS: COMPARING NEEDS AND RESOURCES

Many researchers in SBMH recommend comparing the mapped needs and resources followed by a gap analysis. Cummings and Doll (2008) suggest that this analysis can be conducted by asking the following questions:

- How well are school and community resources integrated?
- Which programs can be eliminated or improved?
- Which services are missing?

PROGRAM SELECTION AND IMPLEMENTATION

Selecting SBMH programs is a complex task. Without a specific data-based process in place, it is difficult to select and plan appropriate evidence-based SBMH services. There is little research available on the best methods for implementing EBP in schools (Hunter, Hoagwood, Evans, Weist, Smith, Paternité, Horner, Osher, & Jensen, 2005). However, as previously stated, the literature on SBMH services almost exclusively promotes a multi-tiered ap-proach, incorporating universal, targeted, and intense services. This approach, by its very nature, first requires careful planning and sound leadership. Then program selection can begin.

A wide variety of EBPs for SBMH interventions are readily available, including several databases that can be accessed on the internet. EBP is a construct that refers to interventions that have met scientific scrutiny. This practice is utilized by several disciplines, including medicine, psychology, and social work. EBP is normally categorized in levels that reflect adherence to certain scientific criteria. Regardless of the numbers of levels, EBP normally includes these key criteria:

- Validity (Does the practice have *internal validity*?)
- Applicability and relevance (Does the practice have *external validity*?)
- Clinical significance (Is the evidence *clinically significant*?)

EVALUATION OF SERVICES AND PROGRAMS (ACCOUNTABILITY)

It is expected that SBMH interventions be evaluated in order to determine whether or not the intervention is effective, although this is not always part of the implementation process. At the very least, interventions should measure outcomes. Many evidence-based interventions already include efficacy measures. It is important to ensure that the people completing these measures (e.g., teachers, parents, students) be aware of the purpose of the evaluations and the purposes and goals of the interventions.

Progress Monitoring

In order to adhere to a multi-tiered population-based approach, measures specific to the SBMH intervention should be taken regularly to ensure that the intervention is meeting the agreed-upon expectations of the intervention. This type of evaluation is conducted between the more conventional pre- and post-intervention measures. There are several readily available measures for progress monitoring for SBMH interventions (e.g., AIMSweb, PBIS).

When SBMH intervention does not produce the expected results, more than the intervention itself needs to be scrutinized. Other factors that can contribute to poor or negative outcomes include:

- the training and expertise of the staff implementing the program
- the quality of the collaboration
  - turf issues
  - community-based professionals understanding of school culture
- supervision of the practitioners

Measures were developed to address the quality of school and community collaborations by Mellin, Bronstein, Anderson-Butcher, Amorose, Ball, and Green (2010). These researchers suggest these measures can assist in determining the level of the collaboration's effectiveness and their ability to function and to find strategies for improvement. Their tool, the *Index of Interprofessional Team Collaboration for Expanded School Mental Health*, measures four factors: (1) reflection on process, (2) professional flexibility, (3) newly created professional activities, and (4) role interdependence.

Researchers support integrating mental health measurement with the accountability measures already in use in most school districts, including high-stakes testing. For example, Hartigan (2011) stated that most schools already track information such as test scores and grades. Child and youth mental health agencies also track their own data, generally including presenting problems and treatment outcomes. She suggests that these databases be joined together, somewhat like a "medical record" for children that charts academic progress, as well as interventions and supports outside and inside school for mental health and other needs. Such integrated data systems are already in existence in certain jurisdictions in the United States.

Hartigan (2011) further discusses several issues inherent in such wide-ranging databases. A basic concern is the reluctance of some data gatherers to share sensitive information with other systems. There are also legal barriers such as release of files, sharing consent, and balancing ease of access to student data while maintaining privacy. Solutions to some of these issues may lie in building trust between agencies and schools. Either or both parties may need to be convinced that sharing data can be more efficient (e.g., save money) by eliminating duplication of services and providing information on how to foster student success and child and youth well-being. Trust may be increased by clarifying that mental health agency staff and school personnel can determine which factors to collect.

Timelines for Measurement

The SBMH literature recommends that evaluators allow sufficient timelines (ranging from twelve to eighteen months) for interventions to show significant changes. This is contrary to most schools' normal practice, in which pressure exists to show changes quickly (Domitrovich et al., 2009). Research on integrating services for children and youth has identified several different outcome measures and the time required to realize expected outcomes (Sebian, Mettrick, Weiss, Stephan, Lever, & Weist, 2007). Examples include the following factors:

- Improved school achievement (>18 months)
- Improved school attendance (18 months)
- Decreased suicide attempts (12 months)
- Decreased utilization of inpatient mental health facilities (>18 months)
- Sustaining mental health improvements (>18 months)
- Reduction in juvenile detention placements (18 months)

Evaluation of Treatment Integrity/Intervention Fidelity

Treatment fidelity, or *intervention integrity*, are terms that may be new to many educators as well as mental health professionals. They are defined as the "extent to which essential intervention components are delivered in a comprehensive and consistent manner by an interventionist trained to deliver the intervention" (Sanetti & Kratochwill, 2011, p. 448).

There are several models of treatment integrity, and according to Sanetti and Kratochwill (2011), they all share the following dimensions:

- Content: Which intervention steps were implemented?
- Quality: How well was the intervention implemented?
- Quantity (also referred to as dosage): How much of the intervention was implemented?
- Process: How was the intervention implemented?

Sanetti and Kratochwill (2011) identify two methods of measuring treatment integrity/fidelity. In the case where SBMH professionals provide direct service to students, one measure of treatment integrity is required. In the other case, when SBMH professionals provide indirect service through teacher consultation, two measures are required: (1) the treatment integrity of the consultation process and (2) the treatment integrity of the delivery of the intervention by the consultee (often an educator).

Treatment integrity is not often included in research reports, particularly those related to child and youth mental health intervention. This could be the result of SBMH practitioners not being aware of the importance of measuring treatment integrity, or the lack of sufficient time and support required to measure treatment integrity. Furthermore, feasible and effective measures of treatment integrity are not readily available; most that exist are specific to particular interventions (Sanetti & Kratochwill, 2011).

It is important to remember that treatment integrity is not always directly related to treatment outcome. Low levels of treatment integrity are not necessarily related to poorer outcomes. SBMH interventions require flexibility within fidelity. For example, a ten-session intervention for anxious students developed in a university lab may need to be adjusted to eight sessions to fit in with the school semester. However, the session content does not change, providing the intervention fidelity.

Sustainability of SBMH Services

The research in SBMH emphasizes that interventions must plan for sustainability because schools are such fluid environments. Within a school district, there normally are numerous changes of administrators, teachers, and even students. Cummings and Doll (2008) identified six steps to address SBMH intervention sustainability. They are as follows:

1. Continual professional development needs with sufficient time and resources allocated
2. Continuous improvement through evaluation of SBMH services with multiple measures
3. Development of infrastructure regarding leadership, personnel, and policies to ensure attainment of SBMH goals
4. Population-based principles and practices integrated into school district structure and processes
5. Clear and documented planning systems and SBMH service implementation understood by all stakeholders
6. Development of communication structures to exchange information with all stakeholders regarding SBMH interventions

In this chapter, we have presented the SISSM Framework for the provision of SBMH services in school districts. Within this framework, we provided a summary of the research and current practice landscape pertaining to SBMH services.

CHAPTER 3

Key Features within the SISSM Framework

Based on the research literature in SBMH, this chapter provides what we believe are necessary guidelines that lead to intervention implementation within the SISSM Framework. These guidelines include procedures for developing SBMH governance, funding, accountability, system change protocols, a multi-tiered approach, and training.

SISSM Framework for SBMH Intervention							**GOVERNANCE**
Governance	Funding	Accountability	System Change Protocols	Multi-tiered Approach	Training	Implementation Process	

When planning integrated SBMH services, it is imperative that a governance body is developed. There are four levels of governance required to implement integrated SBMH services through the SISSM Framework. The first two, the Child and Youth Cabinet and the SBMH secretariat, are at the state/provincial/regional level; and the last two, the School District Mental Health Committee (SDMHC) and the School-based Collaboration Group (SCG), are at the school district level. These levels are presented in figure 3.1, in a jurisdiction where, for example, there are three school districts. Each school district would have one SDMHC. In this jurisdiction, under this secretariat, one SDMHC would have as many SCGs as required. In this case, there are three SCGs in the first district and two in each of the others.

Although some SBMH services do not set up and utilize such a formal body, as illustrated in figure 3.1, in our opinion, establishing and utilizing a clear and well-planned governance structure is a key component in ensuring functional and effective SBMH services. Similar to the current SBMH landscape, we therefore propose a three-level system of governance.

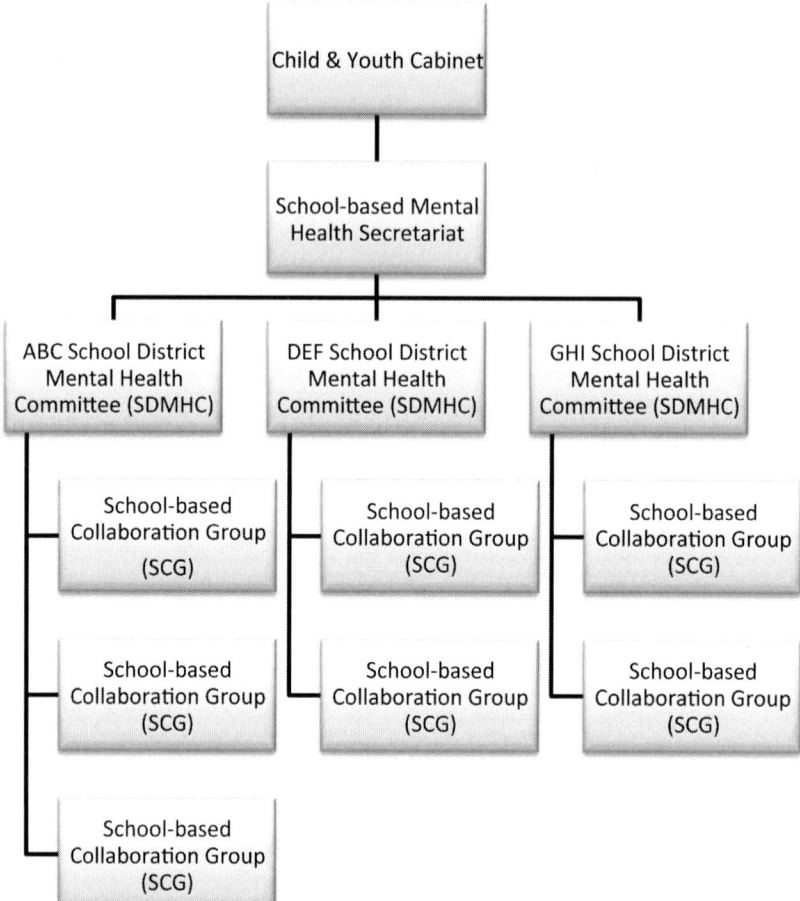

Figure 3.1.   Levels of Governance in the SISSM Framework

State/Provincial/Regional Level

As discussed in chapter 2, many jurisdictions have developed a distinct high-level governmental body that includes representatives from child-serving departments. We suggest that each state, province, or region develop a similar entity to facilitate the implementation of integrated intervention for children and youth in schools, particularly for SBMH services. This decision-making body could be referred to as the Child and Youth Cabinet. Several lists of possible departments for a Child and Youth Cabinet are provided in chapter 2.

Child and Youth Cabinet

In order to ensure stability and sustainability of personnel and interventions, the Child and Youth Cabinet must be legislated into existence. Such legislation would ensure the existence of the Child and Youth Cabinet and give it the authority to pool funding and enact its own legislation regarding services for children and youth.

Another role for the Child and Youth Cabinet could be the development of state/province/regional-wide consensus and policies concerning child and youth mental health. Consensus is required on issues such as the nature and incidence of child and youth mental health disorders. Policy is required on how to address them effectively and efficiently. Our suggestion is that the cabinet involves parents and youth with lived experience with mental health issues when setting policy.

An additional role for the Child and Youth Cabinet could be to mandate the services of multi-disciplinary support services personnel in schools. A minimum complement of these professionals should be employed by school districts. Part of these professionals' role could include the coordination of integrated SBMH services as members of the core group within SISSM, as stated in chapter 1.

Another role for the Child and Youth Cabinet could be the support of appropriate preservice training for graduating mental health professionals who work directly with children and youth. We support a specialty in SBMH services at postsecondary training institutions that graduate professionals in the mental health field.

SBMH Secretariat

The Child and Youth Cabinet could be responsible for establishing the next level of governance, which in essence is an SBMH governance entity at the state, provincial, or regional level. We suggest establishing a secretariat-type governing entity, and it could be referred to as the SBMH secretariat. The secretariat would provide sustainable permanent funding and support training for and evaluation of all SBMH services.

One of the reasons we chose to include this type of entity in the SISSM Framework is that it is important that all stakeholders in SBMH work with a single vision and within a clearly defined structure. We feel that a single vision cannot be achieved fully without the existence of an overarching entity such as the secretariat. The secretariat can more efficiently and inexpensively provide school districts with standards, guidelines, and even templates for implementation. The secretariat would serve to counter the common practice of allowing school districts to plan and develop SBMH interventions independent of each other. This would further serve to avoid duplication of service and eliminate needless expenditures. However, the secretariat should still allow school districts the necessary independence to tailor services to their particular needs.

We see the secretariat as similar in role and function to the governing bodies that exist in some jurisdictions to support student literacy and numeracy development. The secretariat, with the appropriate staff, will also be responsible for the management of the implementation of the SISSM Framework. Appropriate staff would include professionals from the academic and mental health fields who have upper-level management training and experience. The secretariat will guide and facilitate the coordination and integration of SBMH services.

Here we suggest that the secretariat have seven main functions, based on the six categories mentioned in the SBMH literature reviewed in chapter 2. These functions are expanded below to provide clear guidelines for the development of the secretariat's role and functions.

1. Establish and oversee the SBMH accountability system
2. Provide and manage necessary funding
   a. Set up and oversee a system for SBMH expenditures
   b. Provide start-up and, where required, ongoing funding to SDMHCs, and in turn, SBMH core groups
   c. Provide sustainable funding flexible enough to withstand changes in governments and personnel
3. Build readiness for change and support new systems
   a. Create new policies or support existing policies for SBMH to operate within the SISSM Framework
   b. Where required, support the change to MTSS approaches through communication and training with appropriate stakeholders in the educational system and key community organizations within the SISSM Framework
4. Provide and support training for SBMH service providers
   a. Ensure that SBMH personnel have the proper credentials for their roles
   b. Provide and financially support all postservice training activities for school-based support services professionals and the particular community organization-based mental health professionals that will be linked with schools

    c. Provide and financially support required postservice training for educators (both administrators and teachers) within the SISSM Framework

5. Manage implementation of integrated SBMH services
   a. Financially support school districts in the integration of school and community mental health services
   b. Train and provide coaches to assist school districts in the implementation of the SISSM Framework; coaches should have experience in the provision of SBMH services; these coaches could be responsible for working with a predetermined number of school districts based on student population
   c. Mandate that a core group of school-based district/board-employed mental health professionals be available to each school, at least part time, to lead the integration of SBMH services
   d. Mandate that community organizations redeploy sufficient personnel to work with school-based district-employed support services professionals to provide appropriate SBMH services; this should be done without compromising services within their own organization

6. Provide and support data networks for implementation of SBMH services
   a. Perform practice scans in school districts to collect and disseminate current effective practice in SBMH (knowledge exchange)
   b. Support adaptation (while maintaining treatment integrity) of lab-developed evidence-based practices for the fluid and complex school environment
   c. Develop standardized systems for collecting, storing, analyzing, and displaying required data (potentially web-based) that are time efficient and easy to implement for the following:
      i. Needs and resource mapping
      ii. Gap analysis
      iii. Billing systems (third party) where required
   d. Develop a "menu" of multi-tiered culturally sensitive evidence-based SBMH services; facilitate access through existing practice databases (e.g., the Substance Abuse and Mental Health Services Administration)
   e. Develop and distribute SBMH goals template for mental health intervention planning
   f. Support and (when required) develop measures of screening, progress monitoring, outcome (efficacy) and treatment fidelity (see chapter 4)

7. Establish knowledge exchange, translation, and mobilization

   a. Communicate regular updates to policymakers and government decision-makers on SBMH progress
   b. Facilitate collaboration among government, universities, schools, and community organizations for postservice training in SBMH
   c. Regularly examine innovative SBMH practices for possible utilization
   d. Develop and lead conferences to enable knowledge exchange and mobilization

School District–Level Governance

An overarching body for mental health services in each school district should exist, and we suggest it be called the School District Mental Health Committee (SDMHC). The SDMHC would report to the school district's senior management according to the district's structure. This committee would provide a senior management reporting level for all SBMH activities that are generated by the local SBMH collaboration groups (see the SCG section below). The SDMHC is responsible for developing, implementing, and evaluating a school district mental health strategic plan, or reviewing it if it already exists.

Suggestions for membership in the SDMHC include the following individuals who are employed by the school district:

- Senior administration (e.g., the superintendent responsible for student support services)
- School district trustee
- Senior manager of school-based district-employed mental health services (e.g., social work, psychology)
- At least one district-hired mental health coordinator (depending on size of school district)

Where professional associations or unions exist, representation on the SDMHC should be considered.

Responsibilities of SDMHC

- Hire and oversee school district mental health coordinator(s) position
- Develop, implement and evaluate the school district mental health strategy and modify as necessary (which can be incorporated into the school district's strategic plan)
- Implement system change protocols at the school district level for integration of SBMH as part of the school district mental health strategy

- Determine number of SCGs; set up and maintain local SCGs based on high schools and their feeder schools or other configurations
- Create memoranda of agreement for collaborative relationships with community organizations for the provision of services (may be done at the SCG level where applicable)
- Provide decision-making authority for redeployment of certain staff (e.g., SBMH professionals) when required by the SCG
- Provide computer-based supports for data-based decision-making for mental health interventions
- Address accountability issues from SCGs
- Select, train, and support School mental health Core Representatives (SCRs). These individuals are the core group of school-based district-employed mental health professionals as stated in the description of SISSM in chapter 1. These professionals are a subset of all school-based district-employed mental health professionals. Their role is to
  - Be a member of an SCG
  - Present SISSM Framework planning tools to their school's SCG
  - Oversee, collaborate, and deliver integrated SBMH services within the SISSM Framework

School District-hired Mental Health Coordinator(s) Responsibilities

Each school district should employ a qualified mental health professional for the SBMH coordinating position. This individual should be a credentialed SBMH professional with managerial experience. Their role would include the following:

- Act as a change agent (for system-wide change) at the district level
- Support SCGs:
  - Facilitate representation on SCGs from each SISSM community organization
  - Assist in developing local SBMH goals from the secretariat
  - Facilitate determination of priorities at the local SCG level
  - Facilitate decisions concerning redeployments of resources
  - Source funds for small projects
- Organize local professional development (postservice) training activities
- Oversee quality management and evaluation processes (e.g., monitor intervention implementation and treatment fidelity)
- Research current evidence-based SBMH interventions

The School-based Collaboration Group (SCG)

As previously stated, the SCG would be developed by the SDMHC. The SCG should be given a high degree of autonomy in order to implement efficient locally based SBMH services. Within a school district, there may be multiple locally based SCGs, depending mainly on the size and student population of the school district. There could be one SCG per school or one for a small group of schools, as illustrated in figure 3.1. In very small school districts, it is conceivable that the SCG can be the SDMHC.

When developing the initial group of SCGs, it is important to invite representatives from the six categories of community organizations identified in the SISSM Framework:

1. community mental health
2. community health and allied health
3. social services agencies
4. youth justice services
5. local organizations
6. universities/colleges

Below we include suggestions for school members of a local SCG:

- School district administrator
- SCR
- School nurse (where available)
- District-based allied health professionals (e.g., speech-language pathologists, occupational therapists)
- Special education teacher(s)
- General education teachers(s)
- District-employed paraprofessionals (e.g., teaching assistants)
- Guidance and other specialty teachers
- Crisis, safe schools, transition support staff
- Student and parent representation—PTA/parent councils, family engagement teams

Below we include suggestions for community members of a local SCG:

- Community child and youth mental and addiction services (e.g., children's mental health agency, substance abuse treatment intervention)

- Community health and allied health (e.g., hospital inpatient unit staff, hospital mental health outpatient service staff, public health staff, occupational therapists, physical therapists, speech-language pathologists)
- Social services agencies (e.g., child protection services, immigration settlement services, welfare)
- Youth justice (e.g., courts, probation, corrections, police services, alternative justice programs)
- Local community organizations (e.g., recreation centers, service clubs, community coalitions, cultural and religious institutions, community coalitions including antidrug, poverty, civic leadership, mentoring services, business organizations)
- Universities/colleges (e.g., psychology, social work, youth work, education training programs)

It is our view that the leader of the SCG be a school district-based and employed licensed school mental health professional with special training in meeting facilitation. Such professionals in our opinion are often not only best versed in the education and mental health fields, but they also have the necessary knowledge on how to best deliver mental health intervention and similar programs in schools.

Tables 3.1 and 3.2 provide rosters to complete when developing a SCG. We suggest that particular SCGs be readily identifiable—that is, give itself a title, especially when a school district has more than one SCG. The title can reflect the composition of the SCG—for example, the name of the high school if the SCG is based on a high school and its feeder schools.

Table 3.1 is a roster for the school-based SCG members, and table 3.2 is a roster for the community organization members.

Responsibilities of the SCG

- Determine a common vision and set goals for the provision of SBMH services
- Procure funding if not already provided
- Set up comprehensive accountability system aligned with secretariat and school district–mandated practice and adhere to the process
- Implement system change protocols at the SCG level
- Ensure MTSS
- Ensure that the professionals integrated into the schools have the appropriate training, qualifications, and expertise

Table 3.1.   SCG School Member Roster

SCG: _____ Recorder: _____ Date: _____

Role	Professional Discipline (if applicable)	Name	Contact Information
School district administration			
District-based and employed mental health professionals and/or support services multi-disciplinary teams			
District-based but third-party hired and salaried (where applicable)			
School nurse (where available)			
District-based allied health professionals			
District-employed paraprofessionals (e.g., teaching assistants)			
Special education teacher(s)			
General education teacher(s)			
Guidance and other specialty teachers			
Crisis, safe schools, transition support staff			
Student and parent representation—PTA/parent councils, family engagement teams			
Other			

Table 3.2.   SCG Community Member Roster

SCG: _____ Recorder: _____ Date: _____

Community Organization Category	Specific Community Organization	Professional Discipline (if applicable)	Name of Individual	Contact Information
Community mental health				
Community health and allied health				
Social services				
Youth justice				
Local organizations				
Universities and colleges				

- Ensure supervision is carried out by the appropriate professionals
- If not already implemented by the SDMHC, ensure that there is a district-based and employed school mental health professional in each school who has the responsibility for facilitating and supporting community-based services into the schools (SCR)
- Complete the SBMH implementation process
  - Redeploy and reassign resources to provide SBMH interventions in schools with support of the SDMHC
  - Develop communication systems to disseminate the information required by all stakeholders
  - Develop and implement an effective process for resolving professional differences and disputes

Once the SCG is formed, the terms of reference should be developed and periodically reviewed in order to ensure clarity in roles and responsibilities. Each representative from the six community organizations should be responsible for determining which of their resources are available to be deployed to SBMH intervention. It is helpful for each community organization to share the relevant portions of their strategic plan from the onset at the first SCG. It is important that there be individuals from both the school and the community who have the authority to designate, reassign, and redeploy resources (e.g., administrator at the school level, executive director/manager at the community level). A suggested outline/checklist for development of the terms of reference is in table 3.3.

Memoranda of agreement may also be developed by the SCG when community organizations will be providing services in the schools. These legal documents would normally be produced through the offices of school district senior administrators and community organization management.

Such memoranda may include the following:

- The organizations and any governmental initiative related to the agreement
- The purpose of the agreement
- The time frame of the agreement
- Any previous history of collaboration between the organizations
- Benefits and expectations from both entities
- Interventions and organizations' responsibilities
- Accountability processes
- Alignments with relevant privacy and other legislation
- Details of clinical work

Table 3.3.   SCG Terms of Reference Checklist

SCG: _____ Recorder: _____ Date: _____

☐ Confirm members' names, titles, representation, and contact information

☐ Appoint an alternate for each member to ensure sustainability

☐ Determine term for each member (e.g., staggered three-year terms)

☐ Establish SCG meeting frequency; set dates for the year

☐ Confirm meeting locations and other details (e.g., book meeting rooms; order refreshments, audio-visual equipment; appoint chair, minute taker, communication lead; etc.)

☐ Develop group norms

    ☐ Establish meeting process (e.g., Roberts Rules)

    ☐ Determine conflict resolution process

- Application of standards of clinical practice (e.g., record keeping, privacy legislation, supervision, standards of practice)
- Cost-sharing process(es)
- Allocation of any revenues from third-party payments, if applicable
- Details of process(es) for conflict resolution
- Details of review mechanisms (prioritizing)
- Insurance

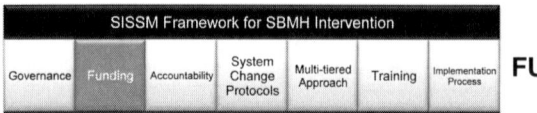 **FUNDING**

Assured and sustained funding for integrated mental health services is paramount for the successful implementation and sustainability of any SBMH intervention. In the SISSM Framework, resources (human and financial) are integrated through relocating and redeployment. In essence, existing human resources from the community are integrated into schools. Therefore, there is often minimal need to procure additional funds to provide integrated mental health services in schools. In addition, salaries may not have to be transferred when resources are being redeployed for school-linked services. When personnel from community institutions are integrated into schools to provide services, the community institution continues to fund their salaries.

In cases where SBMH services are required to expand substantially, or where school-based support services do not yet exist, new funding may be required. As stated in chapter 2, the process of providing SBMH services through grant-based funding is often inefficient and affects direct service sustainability. In addition, providing mental health services in schools through fee-for-service and third-party payers (i.e., insurance) often complicates the process and further reduces the funds and resources that would otherwise be available for direct services. Therefore, we support that governments provide sustained funding for SBMH services.

Where this type of government funding is not available, we provide a list of potential funding sources below.

Potential Funding Sources

- School-based government funding
  - General education funding
  - Special education funding (students who are formally identified through their school system as having mental health issues)

- ○ Internal school support services staff funding if not included above (e.g., psychologists, social workers, counselors)
- ○ Funds for safe schools, anti-drug education, and other programs
- Grants
  - ○ Private foundations
  - ○ Corporate foundations
  - ○ Public foundations (e.g., nongovernmental organizations)
- Reimbursement programs
  - ○ Government-funded health insurance
  - ○ Private insurance

Funding for SBMH may also require funds to provide training. Many school districts, as well as community institutions, have funds set aside for training and/or professional development. Utilizing the SISSM Framework, a certain percentage of these funds could be pooled from school districts and relevant community organizations to enable cross-training in integrated population-based SBMH supports for children and youth.

It is expected that when the SISSM Framework is fully implemented and maintained, the number of students requiring special education services will decrease. Similarly, intense mental health services delivered by community organizations can be expected to decrease. It is important to understand that these potential changes may take several years to be realized. Savings can be redirected to providing additional prevention and early intervention services as well as expanding SBMH services in general.

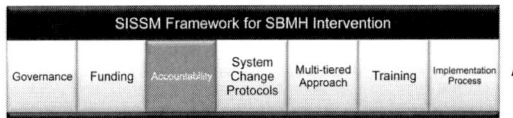 **ACCOUNTABILITY**

Accountability must be an integral component of all levels of SBMH services and must be implemented throughout the planning and delivery and evaluation process. The SBMH services should align with SCG goals and strategic goals of the school district. Specific intervention-level accountability is discussed in chapter 4.

When integrating services, common practice is for the schools and the community organizations to be separately accountable to their governing bodies. There is little, if any, accountability between the schools and their community partners. This situation is depicted in figure 3.2. These current accountability practices are essentially vertical. The vertical paths of accountability are most commonly utilized. However, the current trend for increased integration of

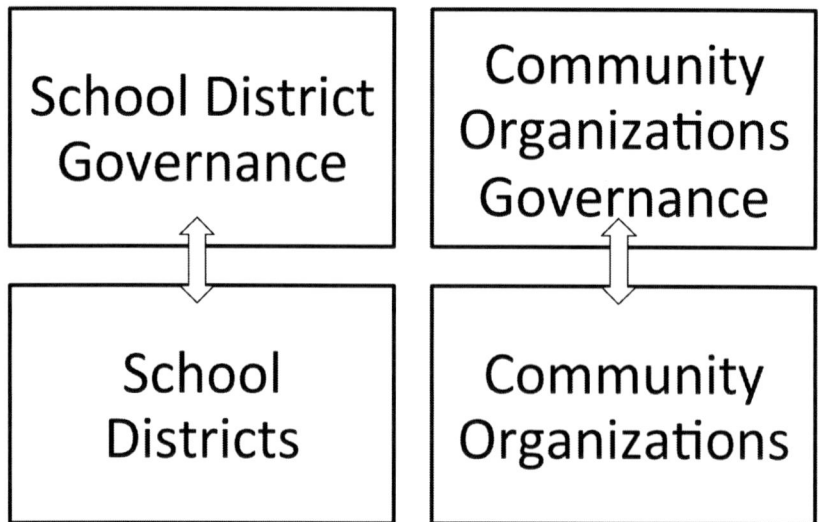

Figure 3.2.   *Common Paths of Accountability: Vertical*

community organizations into schools calls for increased collaboration. As a result, additional paths of accountability should be implemented.

We are proposing the addition of horizontal paths between the community organizations and the school systems, as well as a path between the governing entities. Horizontal accountability is not as formalized as vertical accountability. However, we suggest that there has to be joint accountability systems set up between any two organizations that are working together toward achieving the same goal. This is a variation on Limbrick's (2012) "horizontal teamwork in a vertical world" (as stated in chapter 2). The process of accountability at both the horizontal and vertical levels requires that the practice allows for a certain degree of organizational independence as well as interdependence with integration partners. This is seen in figure 3.3.

When SBMH services are integrated with community organizations, it is necessary to determine who is responsible for the development and adherence to accountability. It is suggested that the organizations and the school system be held jointly responsible for accountability. An important tenet of outcome measures is that change takes a significant amount of time. Therefore, it is expected any short-term accountability measures need to take these timelines into account. For example, it is well documented that positive changes in mental health of children and youth likely take more than an academic year to show results.

Accountability should be an integral part of all roles in SBMH. Therefore, all stakeholders, as appropriate, should be involved in the selection of account-

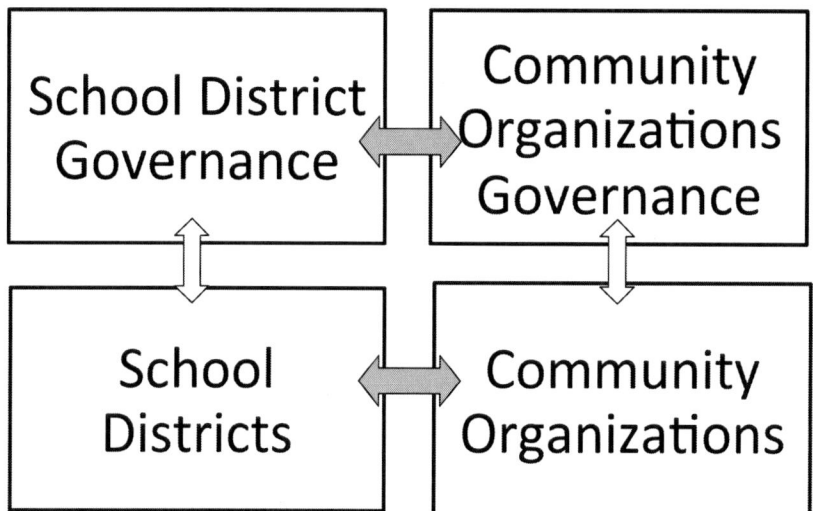

Figure 3.3. *Proposed Paths of Accountability: Vertical and Horizontal*

ability measures. In this way, they are meaningful to the people both gathering the measures and those receiving them. Measures should not be so complex that they require a significant outlay of time and funds. We suggest that the SCG attempt to utilize measures that are already being collected, such as "Office Discipline Referrals," attendance, grades, and other data that are already measured within the school system.

Accountability measures should be valid and reliable. It is important to agree on the directionality of change (e.g., grades will increase and absenteeism will decrease). If possible, comparisons should be included, such as control groups, where the same measures are administered to groups of similar students who are not receiving the intervention in question. It is important to limit the number of evaluation measures; if there are too many, few stakeholders will make the necessary commitment to carrying them out.

Accountability measures can include the following:

- Efficiency of service integration
- Adherence to program standards
  - evidence-based interventions
  - staff-client ratios
- Program outcomes
  - School measures
    - Academic achievement
    - Student behavior (e.g., discipline referrals, suspensions)

- ▪ Attendance
- ▪ School climate
- ○ Mental health measures
  - ▪ Resilience
  - ▪ Mental health symptom reduction
  - ▪ Referrals to and use of in/outpatient facilities
  - ▪ ER visits (may increase initially)
  - ▪ Child and youth mental health facility visits (may increase initially)
  - ▪ Youth justice statistics (long-term measures)
- ○ Cost-effectiveness of programs
  - ▪ Number of students/clients served
  - ▪ Costs per client served
  - ▪ Costs of resources allocated
- ○ Client (students, teachers, parents) satisfaction with
  - ▪ Intervention provided
  - ▪ Staff providing the intervention
- ○ Treatment integrity or fidelity
  - ▪ Direct intervention to service recipient by the SBMH professional
    - • How well the intervention's treatment protocol is followed
  - ▪ Indirect intervention to service recipient where SBMH professional provides consultation to another school staff to administer the intervention
    - • How well the SBMH professional provides consultation
    - • How well the consultee delivers the intervention

In order to ensure effectiveness of SBMH services, accountability must be an integral part of the process. Implementing accountability measures may require additional funds and practitioner time. This increase in funds and time may result in resistance among both practitioners and management. To minimize this resistance, it is important to communicate the purpose of accountability measures to practitioners, managers, and even stakeholders.

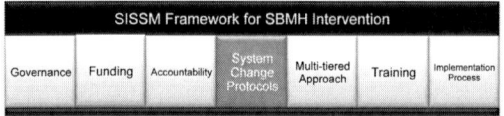

SYSTEM CHANGE PROTOCOLS

Facilitating implementation of integrated SBMH services requires that a systematic process be followed by both the school and the community organizations involved. It is also important that sufficient time and resources are provided for this process. Utilizing concepts from systems change theory, we recommend that both school districts and community agencies designate change agents when implementing a new integrated system. For example, the district mental health coordinator or designated SBMH professional can provide these services in a more general manner for the school district. At the SCG level, we recommend that an SCR be the change agent for individual schools. A similar recommendation is made for the community organizations involved when working in schools. We suggest that a mental health professional assume this role for his or her community organization where applicable.

Table 3.4 provides a guide to support systems change when implementing integrated SBMH services. This guide should be followed by the SCG during the integration and implementation process.

Within the SISSM Framework, protocols for system change require planning for sustainability of new and existing SBMH interventions. The SCG should be prepared to provide updated intervention training for changes in personnel within their SBMH plan. Resistance to change can be minimized by addressing certain parameters of integration on an ongoing basis. These parameters include, but are not limited to, supervision, roles, evaluation, communication, and professional conflicts as well as operational issues.

SISSM Framework for SBMH Intervention						
Governance	Funding	Accountability	System Change Protocols	Multi-tiered Approach	Training	Implementation Process

MULTI-TIERED APPROACH

As stated in chapter 2, MTSS are a common practice in SBMH. The SCG is responsible for the implementation process, which includes needs and resource mapping and gap analysis, as detailed in chapter 4. This process can be facilitated by the SDMHC through the mental health coordinator at the district level. Within the schools, the SCR can play a key role in choosing interventions appropriate to individual schools. To assist in choosing appropriate interventions, we provide a list of intervention types for each tier in table 3.5. As detailed in chapter 4, there are numerous databases of evidence-based interventions online from which to choose after the schools have determined the categories and tiers of interventions.

It is important for all involved in integrated SBMH interventions to understand that schools do not continuously require services at all tiers. Regularly scheduled needs and resource-mapping activities will determine which services are required. In addition, SBMH services are not just for students; they can include interventions for educators and families of students.

Table 3.4. SISSM Framework System Change Implementation Checklist

SCG: _____ Recorder: _____ Date: _____

☐ Obtain the support of key leaders in school district and community organizations

☐ Prepare school-based district-employed mental health professionals to work collaboratively with the selected community organizations

☐ Prepare other school personnel (e.g., teachers, administrators) for integration of community organizations into schools

☐ Prepare selected community organization personnel for integration into school settings

☐ Ensure that all stakeholders understand the relationship between mental health and academic achievement

☐ Ensure consistency and acceptance of "messages" to schools and community organizations regarding the relevance and benefits of the integration and the selected programs

☐ Communicate consistent descriptions and details of the planned programs to stakeholders

☐ Facilitate evaluation of initial implementation to make minor adjustments

☐ Communicate results of progress monitoring to stakeholders

☐ Communicate evaluation results to stakeholders

☐ Support procedures to ensure sustainability

    ☐ Ensure a core group of school-based district-employed SBMH professionals to assist in coordinating integrated programs

    ☐ Provide relevant training, preferably through a "train-the-trainer" model

    ☐ Implement cost-effective SBMH programs, where applicable

    ☐ Monitor personnel changes and plan for succession

Table 3.5.   List of Intervention Types for Multi-tiered Systems of Support

TIER 1: UNIVERSAL

- Mental health awareness
- Mental health literacy
- Stigma reduction
- Social-emotional learning
- Cultural awareness
- Classroom and behavioral management
- Peer mediation
- Family engagement
- Positive parenting
- Crisis response training
- Restorative justice
- Substance abuse prevention
- Suicide prevention
- Violence prevention

TIER 2: TARGETED

- Teacher consultation
- Group programs for students with
  - emerging MH issues
  - academic needs
  - behavior needs
- Group programs for parents of
  - at-risk students
  - exceptional students
- Mentor programs
- Drop-out prevention
- Functional behavioral assessment

TIER 3: INTENSE

- Crisis response and management
- Individual and group intervention
- Case management
- Threat assessment and management
- Transition support for students in treatment
- Special education class support
- Suspension and expulsion programs
- Symptom-monitoring for students in pharmacological treatment

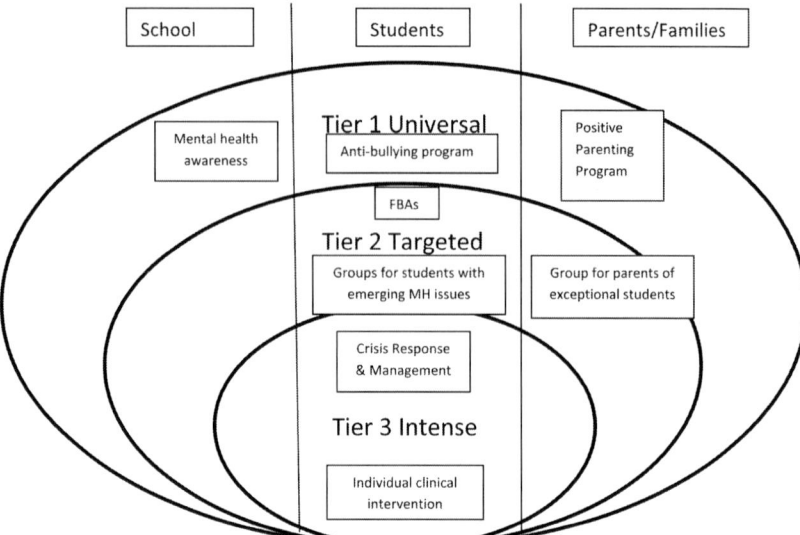

Figure 3.4. *Examples of Multi-tiered Systems of Support: Categories of Intervention for SBMH*

Figure 3.4 illustrates the types of intervention that can be applied at each tier for students, schools staff, and parents and families. In this example, the most recent needs and resource-mapping activity determined that intervention at each tier for students, school staff, and parents and families was not required. This may well change after the next mapping activity.

SISSM Framework for SBMH Intervention						
Governance	Funding	Accountability	System Change Protocols	Multi-tiered Approach	Training	Implementation Process

TRAINING

There are certain competencies that are required for mental health professionals to practice in schools. However, as mentioned in chapter 2, research has shown that some mental health professionals are graduating out of their postgraduate programs without specific training in SBMH practice. In view of current trends to integrate SBMH services, we feel that this is an area that requires immediate attention at the postgraduate program level. In the meantime, we suggest that the secretariat assume the responsibility for providing sufficient postservice training for SBMH professionals who require it. This training could include the competencies listed below.

**Expected Competencies for School-based District-Level
Mental Health Professionals**

- Knowledge of working in complex systems (i.e., school settings) with a diverse multi-disciplinary team that includes the following:
  - Teachers
  - Administrators
  - Educational consultants
  - Other support services professionals
  - Families
  - Representatives from community institutions
- Ability to work flexibly in the fluid school environment
- Knowledge of connection between academic achievement and mental health issues
- Knowledge of current educational initiatives including, but not limited to
  - Education legislation
  - District and school improvement plans
  - Literacy and numeracy reforms and processes
  - High-stakes testing
- Knowledge of school culture and school climate issues
- Knowledge of MTSS approach to SBMH intervention, including risk and protective factors in student achievement and resiliency
  - Knowledge of needs and resource mapping
  - Data-based decision-making for determining and monitoring progress of evidence-based practice
  - Treatment integrity
  - Progress monitoring
  - Pre- and post-intervention measures
- Knowledge of cultural differences in learning and behavior

In addition, school-linked mental health professionals (from community organizations) redeployed to work in schools through the SISSM Framework may also require specific training regarding school-based services. This can be facilitated through the school districts, or the SCG, or their particular organization. Such training may include the following:

- How to carry out clinical work in a nonclinical setting
- Understanding the relationship between academic problems and student mental health

- Understanding school culture and school climate
- Understanding school system organizational structure
- Understanding school-based district-employed multi-disciplinary team roles and functions
- Understanding educational personnel roles and functions
- Understanding school system and integration accountability processes

Training for Educators

The secretariat can also support state/province/region-wide initiatives in mental health training for educators, such as mental health awareness and literacy. However, this may also be the responsibility of the school districts and/or SCGs within the districts, as determined through their district mental health strategy.

In order to ensure the highest uptake of training for all participants, the following training methods should be considered: (1) embedded professional development that is paired with ongoing networks, (2) study groups or professional learning communities, (3) alignment of training with local school goals and standards, and (4) mentoring or coaching during early implementation and school/class-level support throughout. It is important that the suggested professional development not be viewed as an additional obligation; it must be coordinated with preexisting programs as well as participants' previous training and background knowledge.

This chapter has provided a detailed guide for system-level structures within the SISSM Framework, specifically governance, funding, accountability, system-change protocols, multi-tiered approach, and training.

CHAPTER 4

SISSM Framework
SBMH Implementation Process

The present chapter provides the tools necessary for SCGs to implement SBMH services within the SISSM Framework. These tools are completed by each school in an SCG. Then the completed tools are presented to the SCG implementation planning meeting by the SCRs, as stated in chapter 3.

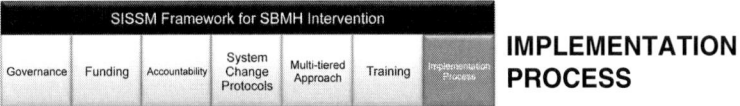

IMPLEMENTATION PROCESS

Figure 4.1 illustrates the four steps in the implementation process of the SISSM Framework that the SCG must utilize to implement SBMH services:

A. Map and prioritize school-based needs
B. Map resources: personnel
C. Map resources: programs
D. Plan SBMH interventions

Map and Prioritize School-based Needs

There are numerous sources that can provide the necessary data to determine school needs through a mapping activity. We have divided these data sources into four categories. It is important to note that the data collected will generally be aggregate in nature based on information gathered from the school communities in the SCG.

- School academic data
- School mental health services data

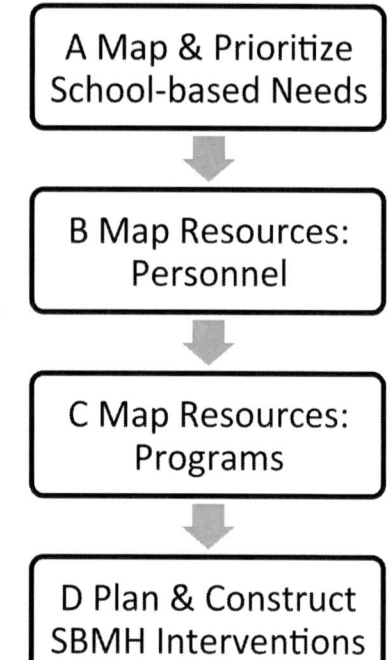

Figure 4.1. *Steps in the SISSM Framework Implementation Process*

- Local school community mental health services data
- Local school community demographic data

We have provided a template for each of these categories of data to assist the SCGs in mapping SBMH needs. Each template has two parts: on the left are the major classifications of the data sources, and on the right, within each classification, are suggestions of specific data that can be collected to determine priority concerns and SBMH needs. At the end of each classification, there is a space to document the priority concern. We suggest that the SCG appoint members to collect the data. In some districts, the SDMHC will be able to provide or assist in collecting these data. This information is brought to the next meeting of the SCG by the SCR to establish the priority needs. We caution that SCGs do not have to collect data from all of the four categories. Schools can decide on which data to collect based on their understanding of their school's SBMH needs.

Table 4.1 is the template (Tool A-1) for mapping needs from the academic data from each school in the SCG.

Table 4.2 is the template (Tool A-2) for mapping needs from the SBMH services data from each school in the SCG.

Table 4.1.   SISSM Framework Tool A-1: Mapping Needs—General School Data

School: _____ SCG: _____ Recorder: _____ Date: _____

Classification	Data
School Academic Data	• Mandatory academic testing data • Grades • Credit accumulation rates for high school • Drop-out rates (high school) • Other (specify) • Priority concern:
Special Education Data	• Number of students with exceptionalities • Number of students receiving special education services that are not formally identified • Number of students on waiting lists for service • Priority concern:
Emotional/Behavioral Occurrence Data	• Current academic year (number and descriptions) • Previous academic year (number and descriptions) • Priority concern:
School Discipline Data	• Office discipline referrals (number and descriptions) • Suspensions (number and descriptions) • Recurring suspensions (number and descriptions) • Expulsions (number and descriptions) • Priority concern:
Absenteeism Data	• Students with prolonged absences (number and reasons) • Students with numerous lates (number and reasons) • Priority concern:

Table 4.2. SISSM Framework Tool A-2: Mapping Needs—School Mental Health Services Data

School: _____ SCG: _____ Recorder: _____ Date: _____

Classification	Data
School Multi-Disciplinary Team Case Data	• Reasons for referrals • Nature of problems/diagnoses • Nature and duration of intervention • Concerns requiring additional intervention • Other (specify) • Priority concern:
School Mental Health Practice Scan	• Universal MH promotion and MH prevention • Targeted prevention for students at risk and early intervention for emerging MH disorders • Intense intervention and chronic care for students with high needs • Priority concern:

Survey Data	• Survey Type: MH School Climate Other (specify)
	• Respondents: Students Teachers Administrators Parents Support staff Other (specify)
	• Priority concerns:
	  ○ Type: Respondent: Concern:
	  ○ Type: Respondent: Concern:
	  ○ Type: Respondent: Concern:

Screening Data	• Student pathology (e.g., anxiety, depression) • Student resilience (e.g., social competence) • Other (specify) • Priority concern:

Table 4.3 is the template (Tool A-3) for mapping needs from the mental health data from the community around each school in the SCG.

Table 4.4 is the template (Tool A-4) for mapping needs from the demographics data from the community around each school in the SCG.

After all the templates have been completed by the school, Tool A-5 is completed. The priority concerns from tools A-1 to A-4 (tables 4.1–4.4) are recorded under the needs classifications. Next, the school prioritizes three mental health needs.

Screening Issues

Table 4.2 (Tool A2) includes mental health screening for schools. As stated in chapter 2, we recommend alternatives to screening, such as using resilience or positive-based measures. If student mental health screening is utilized, certain cautions must be taken. It is vitally important that schools follow a specific mental health screening process as well as utilize the appropriate personnel to carry out the screening procedures. Also, mental health screening tools can be incorporated into the referral process for individual students. For example, teachers, parents, and students can complete these screening tools to provide preliminary data and current levels of functioning for the professional who will be assessing the student. Table 4.6 (Tool A-6) provides a checklist for schools when implementing screening measures as part of the mapping needs activities.

When the multiple-gating screening system is complete, mental health intervention should be made available for students who are determined by the clinical interview to have the mental health problem identified by the screening measure (true positives). The school must ensure that there are sufficient mental health professionals available to offer intervention for these students.

The following websites provide some searchable lists of screening tools:

1. http://www.excellenceforchildandyouth.ca/about-learning-organizations/measures-database
2. http://www2.massgeneral.org/schoolpsychiatry/screeningtools_table.asp
3. http://www.cebc4cw.org

Mapping Resources

Mapping resources requires gathering information regarding both personnel and interventions or services at the school and community level. A key

**Table 4.3.   SISSM Framework Tool A-3: Mapping Needs—Community Mental Health
Services Data**

School: _____ SCG: _____ Recorder: _____ Date: _____

Classification	Data
Referral Data	• Reasons for referral • Nature of problems/diagnoses • Availability of mental health intervention facilities • Other (specify) • Priority concern:
Intervention Data	• Interventions used • Duration of interventions • Priority concern:
Wait List and Wait Time Data	• Average wait time • Number of cases on wait lists • Other (specify) • Priority concern:

Table 4.4. SISSM Framework Tool A-4: Mapping Needs—Community Demographics Data

School: _____ SCG: _____ Recorder: _____ Date: _____

Classification	Data
Social and Economic Data	• Cultural diversity • Average income level • Percent below poverty line • Percent adult and youth unemployment • Amount and nature of criminal activity in area • Other (specify) • Priority concern:
Immigration Data	• Percent recent immigration • Percent ESL • Other (specify) • Priority concern:
Family Data	• Percent of single parents • Percent of seniors • Number household moves and reasons • Other (specify) • Priority concern:
Education Data	• Percent high school drop-outs • Percent high school graduates • Percent postsecondary graduates • Other (specify) • Priority concern:

Table 4.5. SISSM Framework Tool A-5: Mapping Needs—Summary and Priority Planning

School: _____ SCG: _____ Recorder: _____ Date: _____

General School Data		School MH Services Data		Community MH Services Data		Community Demographics Data	
Classification	Priority Concern	Classification	Priority Concern	Classification	Priority Concern	Classification	Priority Concern
School academic data		School MDT case data		Referral data		Social and economic data	
Special education data		School practice scan data		Intervention data		Immigration data	
Emotional/behavioral occurrence data		Survey data		Wait list and wait time data		Family data	
School discipline data		Screening data				Education data	
Absenteeism data							

Prioritize 3 SBMH Needs

SBMH Priority Needs #1

SBMH Priority Needs #2

SBMH Priority Needs #3

Table 4.6.   SISSM Framework Tool A-6: Process Checklist for Informed Mental Health Screening

School: _____ SCG: _____ Recorder: _____ Date: _____

☐ Determine which screening method to use

    ☐ Positive screening (e.g., resiliency scales)

    ☐ Mental health disorder screening tool

☐ Ensure proper consent is obtained (parent and student)

☐ Determine which time(s) of the school year to screen

☐ Determine which grade(s) to screen

☐ Utilize the multiple-gating screening system

    ☐ Gate 1: Distribute, administer, and score screening measure(s) to the selected population

    ☐ Gate 2: SBMH professionals interpret the screening measure results

    ☐ Gate 3: SBMH professionals clinically interview students who meet the predetermined cut-off point suggesting presence of a particular mental health problem

        ☐ False positives are identified (students meeting cut-off point but do not have a mental health problem)

        ☐ Mental health intervention offered for students who are determined by clinical interview to have a mental health problem

consideration with respect to resource mapping is that the data on which it is based is constantly changing. This process must reflect these changes. Within a school year, we suggest that mapping resources take place at the beginning and possibly midway through the school year.

Mapping Resources: Personnel

The school can begin the process of mapping resources by listing the personnel who are currently available to address student mental health needs. We utilize two classifications of personnel. The first is personnel who are employed by the school district. (An alternate system exists in some jurisdictions, whereby school districts contract a company that provides human resources services, including hiring and payroll, for student support services.) This first classification of personnel could include the following:

- SBMH professionals (psychologists, social workers, youth counselors)
- School-based non–mental health professionals (speech-language pathologists, occupational therapists, physical therapists)
- School-based paraprofessionals (teacher assistants)
- Educators/teachers involved in school mental health initiatives (special educators, classroom teachers delivering universal mental health prevention activity)
- Students (student government, peer mediators, tutors)
- Parents (assisting with class trips, parent-teacher association members)
- Volunteers (nonparents who may assist students with reading practice or assistance with organizing activities)

Table 4.7 provides a chart to map the school personnel listed above. This is SISSM Framework Tool B-1. There are sections to list classifications of personnel, the current individuals' names, and their professional discipline, role, and full-time equivalent, where applicable.

The second classification of personnel is in table 4.8. This is Tool B-2, where the school continues mapping resources that are already or could be available for SBMH interventions from the six community organizations listed in the SISSM Framework in their community. There are sections for the type of community organization, the name of the organization, the interventions available, and professional discipline, where applicable. The leaders of the community agencies in the school's SCG need to determine the type of personnel and the amount of time that they can be available to provide services in the schools. This information can be provided to the schools by the SCR who is a member of their SCG.

Table 4.7.   SISSM Framework Tool B-1: Mapping Resources—School Personnel

School: _____ SCG: _____ Recorder: _____ Date: _____

Type	Name	Professional Discipline (if applicable)	Role	FTE
School-based MH professionals (e.g., social workers, psychologists, youth counselors)				
School-based non-MH professionals (e.g., speech-language pathologists, occupational therapists, physiotherapists)				
School-based paraprofessionals (e.g., teaching assistants, educational resource workers)				
Educators (e.g., classroom teachers, special education teachers, consultants)				
Parents				
Students (e.g., peer mediators, tutors)				
Volunteers				
Others				

Table 4.8.   SISSM Framework Tool B-2: Mapping Resources—Community Organizations, Interventions, and Personnel

School: _____ SCG: _____ Recorder: _____ Date: _____

SISSM Framework Community Organization	Name of Organization	Interventions Available	Professional Discipline (if applicable)
Community child and youth mental health and addictions (e.g., mental health clinics, hospital inpatient units, addiction services, crisis response services)			
Community health and allied health (e.g., community health centers, public health system, clinics)			
Social services (e.g., child protection services, community and emergency housing, welfare services)			
Youth justice (e.g., police, probation, corrections, alternative justice services)			
Universities/Colleges (e.g., practica and internship placements for students in psychology, social work, youth counseling, allied health, CYMH research programs)			
Local community organizations (e.g., recreation centers, business, volunteer organizations, faith-based and cultural institutions)			
Other			

The six groups of personnel with examples are listed below:

- Community child and youth mental health and addiction services (e.g., child and youth mental health centers)
- Community health and allied health (inpatient adolescent mental health unit, public health services, early intervention services for speech and language therapy, occupational therapy, physical therapy)
- Social services agencies (e.g., immigration settlement services, welfare, child protection)
- Youth justice (e.g., probation services, youth courts, youth corrections facilities, alternative justice interventions)
- Universities/colleges (e.g., internships from graduate interventions in psychology and social work, placements from youth worker interventions, collaborations for research purposes)
- Local community organizations (e.g., recreation centers; service clubs; community coalitions for anti-drug, safety, cultural and religious institutions; business organizations)

Map Resources: Interventions

The school next maps current interventions with SISSM Framework Tool C-1, called Mapping and Evaluating Current SBMH Interventions. Tool C-1 is completed by the school, except for the decision-making portion, which is determined at an SCG meeting when the information is presented by the SCR. Tool C-1 is depicted in table 4.9.

Tool C-1 has eight columns and is completed by individual schools:

Column 1 depicts the three major tiers of the multi-tiered system of supports, with each subset of supports within the tiers.

Column 2 records the names or types of interventions that are currently being administered within the school.

Column 3 records the personnel classifications utilized to run the interventions listed in Column 2 (e.g., psychologists, social workers, teaching assistants).

Column 4 records the organization responsible for administering the interventions listed in Column 2—namely, the school, the community organization, or both.

Column 5 records the lead personnel responsible for the particular interventions listed in Column 2 and includes the pertinent contact information.

Column 6 records the recipient(s) of the intervention—for example, students, teachers, or parents.

Table 4.9. SISSM Framework Tool C-1: Mapping and Evaluating Current SBMH Interventions

School: _____ SCG: _____ Recorder: _____ Date: _____

Column 1 MTSS Tier	Column 2 Program or Intervention Name or Type	Column 3 Resources Utilized (Personnel— Discipline Classification)	Column 4 School and/ or Community Organization Responsible for Program Intervention	Column 5 Lead Staff Name and Contact Information	Column 6 Program Recipients	Column 7 Program Efficacy (from Tool C-2)		Column 8 Program/Intervention Decision: Continue, Modify, Discontinue	
								8a C M D	8b Justification of Decision and Details of Proposed Modifications
1 Mental health and awareness and mental health promotion						Y	N	C M D	
2 Prevention for students at risk and early identification and intervention for emerging MH disorders						Y	N	C M D	
3 Intense intervention and chronic care for students with serious mental health disorders						Y	N	C M D	

Column 7 records whether or not the intervention meets efficacy criteria. This is determined by an additional tool that is completed for each intervention listed in Column 1.

Column 8 records decisions regarding current interventions. Column 8a records the decisions made regarding each current intervention: continue, modify or discontinue. This decision is made after Tool C-2 is completed for each intervention. Column 8b records the justification for the decision, and records details of any proposed intervention modifications if required.

Tool C-2, Determining Applicability of Current SBMH Interventions, is presented in table 4.10. Tool C-2 is required for deciding whether to continue, modify, or discontinue interventions. It may be necessary for the school to work with the SCG or the SDMHC, such as the mental health coordinator, to assist the schools in completing the C-2 tools.

One of the questions in Tool C-2 is whether or not the intervention is evidence-based. Online databases are available to assist in determining whether or not an SBMH intervention is evidence-based. A list of some of these websites is provided below.

- SAMHSA National Registry of Evidence-Based Programs and Practices (http://nrepp.samhsa.gov): This is a searchable online registry of more than 230 programs for mental health promotion and treatment.
- The Ontario Centre of Excellence for Child and Youth Mental Health (http://www.excellenceforchildandyouth.ca/about-learning-organizations/discover-whats-working/tools/evidence-links): This site provides a list of databases on clinical guidelines and evidence-based practice websites.
- Collaborative for Academic, Social, and Emotional Learning (CASEL) (http://casel.org/publications/safe-and-sound-an-educational-leaders-guide-to-evidence-based-sel-programs): This site provides a downloadable guide rating eighty classroom-based social-emotional learning programs.
- Promising Practices Network (http://www.promisingpractices.net/programs.asp): This site provides summaries of child and youth programs and practices that have been shown to have positive outcomes. Programs are classified by outcome area, indicators, topic, evidence level, and by name alphabetically.
- The UCLA Center for Mental Health in Schools (http://smhp.psych.ucla.edu): Searchable databases are included in this website in the section Practitioner Toolbox, Guides for Practice, Guide for Evidence-Based Practice.

Table 4.10.   SISSM Framework Tool C-2: Determining Applicability of Current SBMH Interventions

School: _____ Recorder: _____ Date: _____

Name/Type of Intervention: _____

Question	Yes/No		Comments
1. Is the intervention choice determined by and meets school needs and connected with district goals and objectives?	Y	N	
2. Is there a clear and objective evaluation process with measures that relate to established district goals and school needs?	Y	N	
3. Is the intervention evidence-based?	Y	N	
4. Is the intervention up to date, or is there a newer evidence-based intervention available that meets the same school needs and district goals?	Y	N	
5. Is the intervention culturally sensitive?	Y	N	
6. Do the personnel delivering the intervention have appropriate training?	Y	N	
7. Are the costs to deliver the intervention reasonable (personnel, time, training costs, material costs)?	Y	N	
8. Does the intervention offer sufficient dosage (e.g., is the intervention duration long enough and frequent enough to be effective)?	Y	N	
9. Is the intervention easily accessible for participants (e.g., participant fees, location, duration, time of day/school year)?	Y	N	
10. Is the intervention well attended?	Y	N	
TOTAL Yes and No	**Y:** **N:**		

In Tool C-2, there are no predetermined cut-off points for the required number of answers to decide if an intervention should continue. It is our opinion that this is best left to the discretion of the school, SCG, or SDMHC.

Plan SBMH Interventions

The remaining tools are completed by the SCG in consultation with each school's administration and relevant staff. Managers of the departments representing school-based district-employed mental health professionals may also be consulted at any point during the planning process.

During a planning meeting, with SCRs from the school, interventions that are being continued or modified should be entered into table 4.11 (Tool D-1), Planning SBMH Interventions.

Column 1 records the applicable SBMH priority need(s) from Tool A-5. These needs should be entered after determining how many of the three priority needs can be addressed in one planning cycle.

Column 2 presents the MTSS classifications. We suggest that interventions be planned for each of these tiers, where possible.

Column 3 records interventions that are being continued or modified from Tool C-1. It is possible that the continued or modified interventions entered from Tool C-1, although beneficial, do not align with the school's identified priority needs. If schools wish to continue programs that do not align with priority needs, and at the same time address priority needs, then additional staff is required. If schools wish to focus only on the priority needs, then the current interventions may have to be discontinued and the personnel from these programs will have to be redeployed to new interventions that address the priority needs. In this situation, or when replacements for previously discontinued interventions are required, the SCG now identifies potential SBMH interventions that are feasible given the resources available (from Tools B-1 and B-2). Redeployment of some personnel from community organizations may also be necessary.

Table 4.12 (Tool D-2), Determining Applicability of Potential Interventions, is provided to assist the planning team when researching new interventions. Tool D-2 needs to be completed for each intervention being considered. Again, it may be necessary for the SCG to work with members of the SDMHC, such as the mental health coordinator, to complete the D-2 tools.

Again, we do not provide cut-off points for scoring the number of Yes and No answers in Tool D-2. It is our opinion that this is best left to the discretion of the planning group, which we suggest is the SCG. After each intervention

Table 4.11. SISSM Framework Tool D-1: Planning SBMH Interventions

School: _____ SCG: _____ Recorder: _____ Date: _____

Column 1 SBMH Priority Need	Column 2 MTSS Tier	Column 3 Intervention Type or Program Name	Column 4 Personnel		Column 5 Intervention/ Program Recipients	Column 6 Intervention/Program Accountability Measures			
			4a School Personnel	4b CO Personnel		6a Alignment with School District Strategic Goal(s)	6b Progress Monitoring	6c Evaluation of Outcomes	6d Intervention/ Program Integrity/ Fidelity
	Tier 1 Mental health literacy and awareness and mental health promotion								
	Tier 2 Targeted prevention for students at risk and early identification and intervention for emerging mental health disorders								
	Tier 3 Intense intervention and chronic care for students with serious mental health disorders								

Table 4.12. SISSM Framework Tool D-2: Determining Applicability of Potential SBMH Interventions

School: _____ SCG: _____ Recorder: _____ Date: _____

Name/Type of Intervention/Program: _____

Question	Yes/No (circle)		Comments
1. Is the intervention evidence-based?	Y	N	
2. Is the intervention culturally sensitive?	Y	N	
3. Does the intervention meet school needs and address district goals?	Y	N	
4. Does the intervention require extensive personnel training?	Y	N	
5. Are there sufficient appropriately trained personnel available to deliver the intervention?	Y	N	
6. Are the costs to deliver the intervention reasonable (personnel, time, training costs, material costs)?	Y	N	
7. Does the intervention offer sufficient dosage (e.g., is the intervention duration long enough and frequent enough to be effective)?	Y	N	
8. Will the intervention be easily accessible for participants (e.g., participant fees, location, duration, time of day/school year)?	Y	N	
9. Does the intervention include a clear and objective evaluation process with measures that relate to established district goals?	Y	N	
TOTAL Yes and No	**Y:** **N:**		

in Column 3 has a Tool D-2 administered, and the Yes and No answers are totaled, the planning team can make the decision about whether or not to utilize the intervention being considered. One of the questions in Tool D-2 is whether or not the intervention is evidence-based. The online databases listed above can also be utilized here to look up potential interventions, or search for suitable interventions given specific SBMH needs.

Column 4 in Tool D-1 records personnel required for the specific interventions, including school personnel (Column 4a) and community organization (CO) personnel (Column 4b).

Column 5 records the recipients of each intervention—for example, students, parents, and teachers.

Column 6 addresses accountability measures, subdivided into four sections.

Column 6a records how interventions align with school district strategic goals.

Column 6b records progress monitoring measures. As stated in chapter 2, progress monitoring consists of measures specific to the intervention that are administered regularly to ensure that the intervention is meeting expectations. Progress monitoring is conducted between pre- and post-intervention measures. These measures are differentiated from outcome measures as they are sensitive to small changes. Many progress monitoring measures are commercially available. In addition, progress monitoring measures are freely available on positive behavior technical assistance websites such as www.pbis.org. Such measures are essential to ensure that the intervention is appropriate for the selected population and that progress is moving toward the expected result.

Column 6c details outcome evaluation, which may include a variety of measures such as the following:

- Measures that come packaged with the particular intervention
- Measures already collected in the school or community (e.g., discipline referrals, ER visits)
- Measures developed by the implementation team

Column 6d records intervention integrity or fidelity measures. These measures ensure that the intervention being delivered is valid and reliable. We suggest the SCG plan measures that refer to the following:

- Intervention content, to ensure that all required intervention steps were implemented
- Intervention quality, to ensure that the intervention adheres to quality standards

- Intervention dosage, to ensure that a sufficient quantity of the intervention was delivered to the selected population
- Intervention process, to ensure that the intervention procedures were implemented appropriately

Measures of treatment integrity should be the responsibility of a supervisor in the same professional discipline. Intervention must be adaptable to the fluidity and complexity of a school district. As stated in chapter 2, throughout planning interventions, the concept of flexibility within fidelity should be followed.

Table 4.13 provides a summary and guide of the SISSM Framework SBMH Implementation Tools with the tool number, tool name, who completes it, and the corresponding table within chapter 4.

This chapter has provided a detailed process for implementing integrated SBMH services from the perspective of a school district local governing group (SCG). It is our opinion that following these specific steps will ensure that integrating SBMH services will be more efficient and effective.

Table 4.13.   SISSM Framework Tools Procedure Guide

Steps	Tool #	SISSM Framework Tool Name	Completed by	Table #
A Map and Prioritize School-based Needs	A-1	Mapping Needs—General School Data	School	4.1
	A-2	Mapping Needs—School Mental Health Services Data	School	4.2
	A-3	Mapping Needs—Community Mental Health Services Data	School	4.3
	A-4	Mapping Needs—Community Demographics Data	School	4.4
	A-5	Mapping Needs—Summary and Priority Planning	School	4.5
	A-6	Process Checklist for Informed Mental Health Screening	School (only if using MH screening measures)	4.6
B Map Resources: Personnel	B-1	Mapping Resources—School Personnel	School	4.7
	B-2	Mapping Resources—Community Organizations, Interventions, and Personnel	School	4.8
C Map Resources: Interventions	C-1	Mapping and Evaluating Current SBMH Interventions	School	4.9
	C-2	Determining Applicability of Current SBMH Interventions	School with district or SCG assistance	4.10
D Plan SBMH Interventions	D-1	Planning SBMH Interventions	SCG	4.11
	D-2	Determining Applicability of Potential SBMH Interventions	SCG with district assistance	4.12

CHAPTER 5

An Illustration of the Process of Implementing the SISSM Framework for SBMH

In *Barriers to Learning*, the process of integrating mental health services into schools was depicted with a narrative example of two classes in a fictional school in a fictional school district. In this chapter, we continue this practice by including examples of the SISSM Framework tools that are planned by a local school and its SCG.

We begin with the formation of one of the district's SCGs. There are three schools in this particular SCG. There is one high school (School A) and two elementary schools (Schools B and C). Tables 5.1 and 5.2 represent the rosters for the school members and community members of the SCG.

After the SCG is formed, each school will complete the SISSM Framework tools independently. We provide an example of each of the SISSM Framework tools completed by School C, one of the elementary schools in this SCG. We are not providing an example of Tool A-6, as it is a checklist.

As stated in chapter 4, it is not necessary for School C to collect data for all the classifications in the Mapping Needs tools (A-1–A-4). These tools provide suggestions of which data to collect. They are not recorded on the tool, but the priority concerns in each classification are entered. Below we provide examples of how School C completed these tools.

School C next summarizes its Mapping Needs tools in SISSM Framework Tool A-5, by first transferring the priority concerns from each completed classification to the corresponding area in Tool A-5. Second, School C sets and records its priority SBMH needs. School C did use a screening tool (measuring student resiliency); therefore, it completed the checklist in Tool A-6. However, we do not include an example here.

The next step is to map resources. First, school personnel resources that are available for SBMH interventions are mapped in Tool B-1. Second, available community organizations personnel and interventions are mapped in Tool B-2.

Mapping and evaluating current SBMH interventions is the next step. School C completes Tool C-1 by listing all of its SBMH interventions, which are provided by the school and the community, and categorizing them within multi-tiered systems of support. In order to complete Columns 7 and 8, they complete Tool C-2 for each of the SBMH interventions listed in Column 1. We provide an example of Tool C-2 for the positive parenting program. After all the C-2 tools are completed, the school decides which interventions will be continued, modified, or discontinued.

The following tools are completed by the SCG. As stated in chapter 4, we recommend that the SCR bring all the completed SISSM Framework tools to an SCG meeting in order to plan SBMH interventions in their school. The SCR will transfer the continuing or modified interventions on to Tool D-1. The SCG then discusses what additional, if any, SBMH interventions will be planned for each school. This may require consultation with the SDMHC, the district mental health coordinator, and other school and community senior management. When new interventions are being considered, Tool D-2 is completed for each potential intervention.

We recommend that the SISSM Framework tools be fully completed in order and by appropriately trained personnel.

Table 5.1.   Example of SCG School Member Roster

SCG:_____ Recorder:_____ Date:_____

Role	Professional Discipline (if applicable)	Name	Contact Information
School district administration	Principal from school A (high school) Principal from school B (elementary)	J.S. W.R.	
District-based and employed mental health professionals and/or support services multi-disciplinary teams	-School Social Worker from school A -Psychologist from school B -Youth worker from school C	M. J. P. Y. D.F.	
District-based but third-party-hired and salaried (where applicable)			
School nurse (where available)	Public health nurse from school C	A.B.	
District-based allied health professionals	-Speech-language pathologist from school B -Occupational therapist from school A	M.W. B.R.	
District-employed paraprofessionals (e.g., teaching assistants)			
Special education teacher(s)	From school B	F.D.	
General education teacher(s)			
Guidance and other specialty teachers	Guidance Counselor from School A (high school)	A. G.	
Crisis, safe schools, transition support staff			
Student and parent representation—PTA/parent councils, family engagement teams	School C PTA representative	J.P.	
Other			

Table 5.2.   Example of SCG Community Member Roster

School: _____ SCG: _____ Recorder: _____ Date: _____

Community Organization Category	Specific Community Organization	Professional Discipline (if applicable)	Name of Individual	Contact Information
Community mental health	Child & Family Mental Health Clinic	Psychologist	D.B.	
Community health and allied health	City Health Center	Family physician	L.N.	
Social services	Family Services Agency	Social Worker	B.Y.	
Youth justice	Probation	Probation officer	D.S.	
Local organizations	Parks & Recreation	Manager of Recreation Center	J.N.	
Universities and colleges	University Psychology Department	Psychology professor	G.C.	

Table 5.3. Example of SISSM Framework Tool A-1: Mapping Needs—General School Data

School: _____ SCG: _____ Recorder: _____ Date: _____

Classification	Data
School Academic Data	• Mandatory academic testing data • Grades • Credit accumulation rates for high school • Drop-out rates (high school) • Other (specify) • Priority concern: _credit accumulation_
Special Education Data	• Number of students with exceptionalities • Number of students receiving special education services that are not formally identified • Number of students on waiting lists for service • Priority concern:
Emotional/Behavioral Occurrence Data	• Current academic year (number and descriptions) • Previous academic year (number and descriptions) • Priority concern: _anxiety_
School Discipline Data	• Office discipline referrals (number and descriptions) • Suspensions (number and descriptions) • Recurring suspensions (number and descriptions) • Expulsions (number and descriptions) • Priority concern:
Absenteeism Data	• Students with prolonged absences (number and reasons) • Students with numerous lates (number and reasons) • Priority concern: _school refusal_

Table 5.4.   Example of SISSM Framework Tool A-2: Mapping Needs—School Mental Health Services Data

School: _____ SCG: _____ Recorder: _____ Date: _____

Classification	Data
School Multi-Disciplinary Team Case Data	• Reasons for referrals • Nature of problems/diagnoses • Nature and duration of intervention • Concerns requiring additional intervention • Other (specify) • Priority concern: _high incidence of anxiety_
School Mental Health Practice Scan	• Universal MH promotion and MH prevention • Targeted prevention for students at risk and early intervention for emerging MH disorders • Intense Intervention and chronic care for students with high needs • Priority concern: _primarily intense intervention_
Survey Data	• Survey Type: MH √ School Climate √ Other (Specify) • Respondents: Students √ Teachers__Administrators__Parents__ Support staff Other (specify) • Priority concerns: • Type: _MH_ Respondent: _students_ Concern: _anxiety_ • Type: _school climate_ Respondent: _students_ Concern: _safety_____ • Type: Respondent: Concern:
Screening Data	• Student pathology (e.g., anxiety, depression) • Student resilience (e.g., social competence) • Other (specify) • Priority concern: _low student resiliency_

Table 5.5.   Example of SISSM Framework Tool A-3: Mapping Needs—Community Mental Health Services Data

School: _____ SCG: _____ Recorder: _____ Date: _____

Classification	Data
Referral Data	• Reasons for referral • Nature of problems/diagnoses • Availability of mental health intervention facilities • Other (specify) • Priority concern: *anxiety most common referral reason*
Intervention Data	• Interventions used • Duration of interventions • Priority concern:
Wait List & Wait Time Data	• Average wait time • Number of cases on wait lists • Other (specify) • Priority concern: *12-month wait list for individual treatment*

Table 5.6.   Example of SISSM Framework Tool A-4: Mapping Needs—Community Demographics Data

School: _____ SCG: _____ Recorder: _____ Date: _____

Classification	Data
Social and Economic Data	• Cultural diversity • Average income level • Percent below poverty line • Percent adult and youth unemployment • Amount and nature of criminal activity in area • Other (specify) • Priority concern: _parent unemployment_
Immigration Data	• Percent recent immigration • Percent ESL • Other (specify) • Priority concern:
Family Data	• Percent of single parents • Percent of seniors • Number of household moves and reasons • Other (specify) • Priority concern: _high number of household moves due to unemployment_
Education Data	• Percent high school drop-outs • Percent high school graduates • Percent postsecondary graduates • Other (specify) • Priority concern:

Table 5.7. Example of SISSM Framework Tool A-5: Mapping Needs—Summary and Priority Planning

School: _____ SCG: _____ Recorder: _____ Date: _____

General School Data Tool A-1		School MH Services Data Tool A-2		Community MH Services Data Tool A-3		Community Demographics Data Tool A-4	
Classification	Priority Concern	Classification	Priority Concern	Classification	Priority Concern	Classification	Priority Concern
School Academic Data	Credit accumulation	School MDT Case Data	high incidence of anxiety	Referral Data	Anxiety most common referral reason	Social and Economic Data	Parent unemployment
Special Education Data		School Practice Scan Data	Primarily intense intervention	Intervention Data		Immigration Data	
Emotional/ Behavioral Occurrence Data	anxiety	Survey Data	-anxiety -safety	Wait List and Wait Time Data	12-month waiting list for individual treatment	Family Data	High # of household moves due to unemployment
School Discipline Data		Screening Data	Low student resiliency			Education Data	
Absenteeism Data	school refusal						

Prioritize 3 SBMH Needs

SBMH Priority Needs #1
Intervention for students with anxiety at school

SBMH Priority Needs #2
Parent supports for students with anxiety at school

SBMH Priority Needs #3
Mental health awareness to school staff, with an emphasis on anxiety

Table 5.8. Example of SISSM Framework Tool B-1: Mapping Resources—School Personnel

School: _____ SCG: _____ Recorder: _____ Date: _____

Type	Name	Professional Discipline (if applicable)	Role	FTE
School-based MH professionals (e.g., social workers, psychologists, youth counselors)	-J.W. (SCR) -T.C. -M.B.	-Psychology -Social Work -Youth Work	-Psychologist -Social Worker -Youth counselor	.2 .4 .5
School-based non-MH professionals (e.g., speech-language pathologists, occupational therapists, physiotherapists)	M.Z. A.D.	-Speech-Language Pathology -Occupational Therapy	-Speech Pathologist -Occupational Therapist	.2 .05
School-based paraprofessionals (e.g., teaching assistants, educational resource workers)	L.M		-Teaching Assistant	1.0
Educators (e.g., classroom teachers, special education teachers, consultants)	Classroom teachers for Tier 1			
Parents	Parent-teacher association members			
Students (e.g., peer mediators, tutors)	Students interested in participating in MH activities in a student leadership role			
Volunteers	Parents and community school volunteers			
Others				

Table 5.9.   Example of SISSM Framework Tool B-2: Mapping Resources—Community Organizations, Interventions, and Personnel

School: _____ SCG: _____ Recorder: _____ Date: _____

SISSM Framework Community Organization	Name of Organization	Interventions Available	Professional Discipline (if applicable)
Community child and youth mental health and addictions (e.g., mental health clinics, hospital inpatient units, addiction services, crisis response services)	Child Mental Health Clinic	Parenting Groups	Social work
Community health and allied health (e.g., community health centers, public health system, clinics)	Public Health	Eating Disorders Awareness	Public Health Nurse
Social services (e.g., child protection services, community and emergency housing, welfare services)			
Youth justice (e.g., police, probation, corrections, alternative justice services)	Community Police Unit	Substance Abuse Awareness	Police Officer
Universities/Colleges (e.g., practica and internship placements for students in psychology, social work, youth counseling, allied health, CYMH research programs)	Local University	Research program on anxiety prevention	Psychology graduate students
Local community organizations (e.g., recreation centers, business, volunteer organizations, faith-based and cultural institutions)	Service Organization	Breakfast program	Organization members
Other			

Table 5.10. Example of SISSM Framework Tool C-1: Mapping and Evaluating Current SBMH Interventions

School: _____ SCG: _____ Recorder: _____ Date: _____

Column 1 MTSS Tier	Column 2 Program or Intervention Name or Type	Column 2 Resources Utilized (Personnel—Discipline Classification)	Column 4 School and/or Community Organization Responsible for Program/Intervention	Column 5 Lead Staff Name and Contact Information	Column 6 Program Recipients	Column 7 Program Efficacy (from Tool C-2)	Column 8 Program/Intervention Decision: Continue, Modify, Discontinue 8a C M D	8b Justification of Decision and Details of Proposed Modifications
1 Mental health and awareness and mental health promotion	-peer mediation	-Youth counselor	-School	M.B.	All students	Y N	C / M / D	Meets applicability criteria, and addresses some needs of students with anxiety
	-positive parenting program	-Social worker	-Child and family mental health clinic	A.D.	Available to all parents in the school	Y N	C / M / D	Does not meet school priority needs
2 Prevention for students at risk and early identification and intervention for emerging MH disorders	Program for primary students with emerging mental health issues	School psychologist and teaching assistant	school	J.W. L.M.	Screened students in kindergarten to Grade 3	Y N / Y N	C / M / D / C / M / D	Meets all applicability criteria, will add personnel to increase available spots in program
3 Intense intervention and chronic care for students with serious mental health disorders	-individual counseling for students with severe mental health issues	-School psychologist -School social worker -Youth counselor	school	J.W T.C. M.B.	Available to students at any grade	Y N / Y N	C / M / D / C / M / D	Does not meet all applicability criteria; modify to introduce evidence-based interventions, particularly for anxiety

Table 5.11.   Example of SISSM Framework Tool C-2: Determining Applicability of Current SBMH Interventions

School:_____ SCG:_____ Recorder:_____ Date:_____

Name/Type of Intervention: *positive parenting program*

Question	Yes/No		Comments
1. Is the intervention choice determined by and meets school needs and connected with district goals and objectives?	Y	<u>N</u>	*School needs programs for students with anxiety*
2. Is there a clear and objective evaluation process with measures that relate to established district goals and school needs?	Y	<u>N</u>	*Evaluation not aligned with district goals or school needs*
3. Is the intervention evidence-based?	<u>Y</u>	N	
4. Is the intervention up to date, or is there a newer evidence-based intervention available that meets the same school needs and district goals?	<u>Y</u>	N	*Program is current with research*
5. Is the intervention culturally sensitive?	<u>Y</u>	N	
6. Do the personnel delivering the intervention have appropriate training?	<u>Y</u>	N	
7. Are the costs to deliver the intervention reasonable (personnel, time, training costs, material costs)?	<u>Y</u>	N	
8. Does the intervention offer sufficient dosage (e.g., is the intervention duration long enough and frequent enough to be effective)?	<u>Y</u>	N	
9. Is the intervention easily accessible for participants (e.g., participant fees, location, duration, time of day/school year)?	<u>Y</u>	N	
10. Is the intervention well attended?	Y	<u>N</u>	
TOTAL Yes and No	**Y: 7** **N: 3**		*Program required to meet needs of students with anxiety & their parents*

Table 5.12. Example of SISSM Framework Tool D-1: Planning SBMH Interventions

School: _____ SCG: _____ Recorder: _____ Date: _____

Column 1 SBMH Priority Need	Column 2 MTSS Tier	Column 3 Intervention Type or Program Name	Column 4 Personnel		Column 5 Intervention/Program Recipients	Column 6 Intervention/Program Accountability Measures			
			4a School Personnel	4b CO Personnel		6a Alignment with School District Strategic Goal(s)	6b Progress Monitoring	6c Evaluation of Outcomes	6d Intervention/Program Integrity/Fidelity
Mental health awareness for school staff with an emphasis on anxiety	Tier 1 Mental health literacy and awareness and mental health promotion	Peer mediation / Mental health awareness training program for school staff	Youth worker / Psychology	Social worker	All students / All staff	Yes / Yes	Add in progress monitoring measures / Add in progress monitoring measures	Expand evaluation measures / Use measures from the awareness training program (staff surveys)	Add in intervention fidelity measures / Supervisors measure fidelity of training program
Parent support for students with anxiety	Tier 2 Targeted prevention for students at risk and early identification and	Program for primary students with emerging mental health issues	Psychologist and Teaching Assistant		Children in primary grades screened with at risk for mental health problems	Yes	Yes, part of program	Yes, part of program	Yes, part of program

| Parent support for students with anxiety | Tier 2 (continued) intervention for emerging mental health disorders | Program for parents of students with anxiety | Social worker | Social worker | Self-identified parents of students with anxiety | Yes | Yes, part of program | Yes, part of program | Yes, part of program |
| Evidence-based intense intervention for students with anxiety | Tier 3 Intense intervention and chronic care for students with serious mental health disorders | Evidence-based intervention for students with anxiety | psychologist | | Students referred for anxiety | Yes | Yes, part of program | Yes, part of program | Yes, part of program by supervisor |

Table 5.13.   Example of SISSM Framework Tool D-2: Determining Applicability of Potential SBMH Interventions

School: _____ SCG: _____ Recorder: _____ Date: _____

Name/Type of Intervention/Program: *program for parents of students with anxiety*

Question	Yes/No (circle)		Comments
1. Is the intervention evidence-based?	Y̲	N	
2. Is the intervention culturally sensitive?	Y̲	N	
3. Does the intervention meet school needs and address district goals?	Y̲	N	*Meets school needs*
4. Does the intervention require extensive personnel training?	Y̲	N	*Yes, but will share costs with children's mental health agency*
5. Are there sufficient appropriately trained personnel available to deliver the intervention?	Y	N̲	*Will need to train some staff, but will use children's mental health agency trainer*
6. Are the costs to deliver the intervention reasonable (personnel, time, training costs, material costs)?	Y̲	N	
7. Does the intervention offer sufficient dosage (e.g., is the intervention duration long enough and frequent enough to be effective)?	Y̲	N	
8. Will the intervention be easily accessible for participants (e.g., participant fees, location, duration, time of day/school year)?	Y̲	N	
9. Does the intervention include a clear and objective evaluation process with measures that relate to established district goals?	Y̲	N	*Excellent accountability measures*
TOTAL Yes and No	**Y: 8** **N: 1**		

Conclusion

In *School-based Mental Health: A Framework for Intervention*, we introduce a comprehensive structure for integrating community-based personnel and programs into school systems. Although the framework utilizes a top-down approach beginning with a state/provincial/regional governing body, it is possible for districts or even schools to begin a comprehensive SBMH intervention process on their own without the presence of such higher-level governance.

In our previous book, *Barriers to Learning: The Case for Integrated Mental Health Services in Schools*, we introduced the School-based Integrated Support Services Model (SISSM) for integrating community organizations into schools for the delivery of mental health services. This model highlights a key integration role allocated to school-based district-employed mental health professionals.

School-based Mental Health expands SISSM by providing a framework based on current research and practice. This framework facilitates the delivery of evidence-based and multi-tiered SBMH interventions that are aligned with school district goals and needs. This is achieved by following a specific yet flexible structure beginning with governance, followed by funding, accountability, system change protocols, a multi-tiered approach, training, and implementation process.

The practice of SBMH should provide a seamless delivery of integrated mental health services to schools. In order to achieve such a goal and maintain such a practice, all practitioners must have expertise in the appropriate field and a sense of determination to work collaboratively while assisting each other in remaining focused on what truly matters—delivering the best possible support services to our students, parents, and schools.

As school districts and community organizations initiate or further develop integrated SBMH services, we encourage practitioners to submit summaries of their SBMH practices and interventions to our website, www. beyondbarrierstolearning.ca. The purpose is to provide a forum for SBMH practitioners, schools and school districts to share successes, challenges and recommendations.

SCG School Member Roster

SCG School Member Roster

SCG: _____ Recorder: _____ Date: _____

Role	Professional Discipline (if applicable)	Name	Contact Information
School district administration			
District-based and employed mental health professionals and/or support services multi-disciplinary teams			
District-based but third-party hired and salaried (where applicable)			
School nurse (where available)			
District-based allied health professionals			
District-employed paraprofessionals (e.g., teaching assistants)			
Special education teacher(s)			
General education teacher(s)			
Guidance and other specialty teachers			
Crisis, safe schools, transition support staff			
Student and parent representation—PTA/parent councils, family engagement teams			
Other			

SCG Community Member Roster

SCG Community Member Roster

School: _____ SCG: _____

Recorder: _____ Date: _____

Community Organization Category	Specific Community Organization	Professional Discipline (if applicable)	Name of Individual	Contact Information
Community mental health				
Community health and allied health				
Social services				
Youth justice				
Local organizations				
Universities and colleges				

SCG Terms of Reference Checklist

SCG Terms of Reference Checklist

SCG: _____ Recorder: _____ Date: _____

☐ Confirm members' names, titles, representation, and contact information

☐ Appoint an alternate for each member to ensure sustainability

☐ Determine term for each member (e.g., staggered three-year terms)

☐ Establish SCG meeting frequency; set dates for the year

☐ Confirm meeting locations and other details (e.g., book meeting rooms; order refreshments, audio-visual equipment; appoint chair, minute taker, communication lead; etc.)

☐ Develop group norms

   ☐ Establish meeting process (e.g., Roberts Rules)

   ☐ Determine conflict resolution process

SISSM Framework System
Change Implementation Checklist

SISSM Framework System Change Implementation Checklist

SCG: _____ Recorder: _____ Date: _____

☐ Obtain the support of key leaders in school district and community organizations

☐ Prepare school-based district-employed mental health professionals to work collaboratively with the selected community organizations

☐ Prepare other school personnel (e.g., teachers, administrators) for integration of community organizations into schools

☐ Prepare selected community organization personnel for integration into school settings

☐ Ensure that all stakeholders understand the relationship between mental health and academic achievement

☐ Ensure consistency and acceptance of "messages" to schools and community organizations regarding the relevance and benefits of the integration and the selected programs

☐ Communicate consistent descriptions and details of the planned programs to stakeholders

☐ Facilitate evaluation of initial implementation to make minor adjustments

☐ Communicate results of progress monitoring to stakeholders

☐ Communicate evaluation results to stakeholders

☐ Support procedures to ensure sustainability

    ☐ Ensure a core group of school-based district-employed SBMH professionals to assist in coordinating integrated programs

    ☐ Provide relevant training, preferably through a "train-the-trainer" model

    ☐ Implement cost-effective SBMH programs, where applicable

    ☐ Monitor personnel changes and plan for succession

List of Intervention Types for Multi-tiered Systems of Support

List of Intervention Types for Multi-tiered Systems of Support

TIER 1: UNIVERSAL

- Mental health awareness
- Mental health literacy
- Stigma reduction
- Social-emotional learning
- Cultural awareness
- Classroom and behavioral management
- Peer mediation
- Family engagement
- Positive parenting
- Crisis response training
- Restorative justice
- Substance abuse prevention
- Suicide prevention
- Violence prevention

TIER 2: TARGETED

- Teacher consultation
- Group programs for students with
  - emerging MH issues
  - academic needs
  - behavior needs
- Group programs for parents of
  - at-risk students
  - exceptional students
- Mentor programs
- Drop-out prevention
- Functional behavioral assessment

TIER 3: INTENSE

- Crisis response and management
- Individual and group intervention
- Case management
- Threat assessment and management
- Transition support for students in treatment
- Special education class support
- Suspension and expulsion programs
- Symptom-monitoring for students in pharmacological treatment

SISSM Framework Tool A-1:
Mapping Needs—General School Data

SISSM Framework Tool A-1: Mapping Needs—General School Data

School: _____ SCG: _____ Recorder: _____ Date: _____

Classification	Data
School Academic Data	• Mandatory academic testing data • Grades • Credit accumulation rates for high school • Drop-out rates (high school) • Other (specify) • Priority concern:
Special Education Data	• Number of students with exceptionalities • Number of students receiving special education services that are not formally identified • Number of students on waiting lists for service • Priority concern:
Emotional/Behavioral Occurrence Data	• Current academic year (number and descriptions) • Previous academic year (number and descriptions) • Priority concern:
School Discipline Data	• Office discipline referrals (number and descriptions) • Suspensions (number and descriptions) • Recurring suspensions (number and descriptions) • Expulsions (number and descriptions) • Priority concern:
Absenteeism Data	• Students with prolonged absences (number and reasons) • Students with numerous lates (number and reasons) • Priority concern:

SISSM Framework Tool A-2: Mapping Needs—School Mental Health Services Data

SISSM Framework Tool A-2: Mapping Needs—School Mental Health Services Data

School: _____ SCG: _____ Recorder: _____ Date: _____

Classification	Data
School Multi-Disciplinary Team Case Data	• Reasons for referrals • Nature of problems/diagnoses • Nature and duration of intervention • Concerns requiring additional intervention • Other (specify) • Priority concern:
School Mental Health Practice Scan	• Universal MH promotion and MH prevention • Targeted prevention for students at risk and early intervention for emerging MH disorders • Intense intervention and chronic care for students with high needs • Priority concern:
Survey Data	• Survey Type: MH School Climate Other (specify) • Respondents: Students Teachers Administrators Parents Support staff Other (specify) • Priority concerns: 　○ Type:　　　　Respondent:　　　　Concern: 　○ Type:　　　　Respondent:　　　　Concern: 　○ Type:　　　　Respondent:　　　　Concern:
Screening Data	• Student pathology (e.g., anxiety, depression) • Student resilience (e.g., social competence) • Other (specify) • Priority concern:

SISSM Framework Tool A-3:
Mapping Needs—Community
Mental Health Services Data

SISSM Framework Tool A-3: Mapping Needs—Community Mental Health Services Data

School: _____ SCG: _____ Recorder: _____ Date: _____

Classification	Data
Referral Data	• Reasons for referral • Nature of problems/diagnoses • Availability of mental health intervention facilities • Other (specify) • Priority concern:
Intervention Data	• Interventions used • Duration of interventions • Priority concern:
Wait List and Wait Time Data	• Average wait time • Number of cases on wait lists • Other (specify) • Priority concern:

SISSM Framework Tool A-4: Mapping Needs—Community Demographics Data

SISSM Framework Tool A-4: Mapping Needs—Community Demographics Data

School: _____ SCG: _____ Recorder: _____ Date: _____

Classification	Data
Social and Economic Data	• Cultural diversity • Average income level • Percent below poverty line • Percent adult and youth unemployment • Amount and nature of criminal activity in area • Other (specify) • Priority concern:
Immigration Data	• Percent recent immigration • Percent ESL • Other (specify) • Priority concern:
Family Data	• Percent of single parents • Percent of seniors • Number household moves and reasons • Other (specify) • Priority concern:
Education Data	• Percent high school drop-outs • Percent high school graduates • Percent postsecondary graduates • Other (specify) • Priority concern:

SISSM Framework Tool A-5: Mapping Needs—Summary and Priority Planning

SISSM Framework Tool A-5: Mapping Needs—Summary and Priority Planning

School: _____ SCG: _____ Recorder: _____ Date: _____

General School Data		School MH Services Data		Community MH Services Data		Community Demographics Data	
Classification	Priority Concern	Classification	Priority Concern	Classification	Priority Concern	Classification	Priority Concern
School academic data		School MDT case data		Referral data		Social and economic data	
Special education data		School practice scan data		Intervention data		Immigration data	
Emotional/behavioral occurrence data		Survey data		Wait list and wait time data		Family data	
School discipline data		Screening data				Education data	
Absenteeism data							

Prioritize 3 SBMH Needs

SBMH Priority Needs #1

SBMH Priority Needs #2

SBMH Priority Needs #3

SISSM Framework Tool A-6: Process Checklist for Informed Mental Health Screening

SISSM Framework Tool A-6: Process Checklist for Informed Mental Health Screening

School: _____ SCG: _____ Recorder: _____ Date: _____

☐ Determine which screening method to use

   ☐ Positive screening (e.g., resiliency scales)

   ☐ Mental health disorder screening tool

☐ Ensure proper consent is obtained (parent and student)

☐ Determine which time(s) of the school year to screen

☐ Determine which grade(s) to screen

☐ Utilize the multiple-gating screening system

   ☐ Gate 1: Distribute, administer, and score screening measure(s) to the selected population

   ☐ Gate 2: SBMH professionals interpret the screening measure results

   ☐ Gate 3: SBMH professionals clinically interview students who meet the predetermined cut-off point suggesting presence of a particular mental health problem

      ☐ False positives are identified (students meeting cut-off point but do not have a mental health problem)

      ☐ Mental health intervention offered for students who are determined by clinical interview to have a mental health problem

SISSM Framework Tool B-1:
Mapping Resources—School Personnel

SISSM Framework Tool B-1: Mapping Resources—School Personnel

School: _____ SCG: _____ Recorder: _____ Date: _____

Type	Name	Professional Discipline (if applicable)	Role	FTE
School-based MH professionals (e.g., social workers, psychologists, youth counselors)				
School-based non-MH professionals (e.g., speech-language pathologists, occupational therapists, physiotherapists)				
School-based paraprofessionals (e.g., teaching assistants, educational resource workers)				
Educators (e.g., classroom teachers, special education teachers, consultants)				
Parents				
Students (e.g., peer mediators, tutors)				
Volunteers				
Others				

SISSM Framework Tool B-2: Mapping Resources—Community Organizations, Interventions, and Personnel

SISSM Framework Tool B-2: Mapping Resources—Community Organizations, Interventions, and Personnel

School: _____ SCG: _____ Recorder: _____ Date: _____

SISSM Framework Community Organization	Name of Organization	Interventions Available	Professional Discipline (if applicable)
Community child and youth mental health and addictions (e.g., mental health clinics, hospital inpatient units, addiction services, crisis response services)			
Community health and allied health (e.g., community health centers, public health system, clinics)			
Social services (e.g., child protection services, community and emergency housing, welfare services)			
Youth justice (e.g., police, probation, corrections, alternative justice services)			
Universities/Colleges (e.g., practica and internship placements for students in psychology, social work, youth counseling, allied health, CYMH research programs)			
Local community organizations (e.g., recreation centers, business, volunteer organizations, faith-based and cultural institutions)			
Other			

SISSM Framework Tool C-1: Mapping and Evaluating Current SBMH Interventions

SISSM Framework Tool C-1: Mapping and Evaluating Current SBMH Interventions

School: _____ SCG: _____ Recorder: _____ Date: _____

Column 1 MTSS Tier	Column 2 Program or Intervention Name or Type	Column 3 Resources Utilized (Personnel— Discipline Classification)	Column 4 School and/ or Community Organization Responsible for Program Intervention	Column 5 Lead Staff Name and Contact Information	Column 6 Program Recipients	Column 7 Program Efficacy (from Tool C-2)		Column 8 Program/Intervention Decision: Continue, Modify, Discontinue	
								8a C M D	8b Justification of Decision and Details of Proposed Modifications
1 Mental health and awareness and mental health promotion						Y	N	C M D	
2 Prevention for students at risk and early identification and intervention for emerging MH disorders						Y	N	C M D	
3 Intense intervention and chronic care for students with serious mental health disorders						Y	N	C M D	

SISSM Framework Tool C-2: Determining Applicability of Current SBMH Interventions

SISSM Framework Tool C-2: Determining Applicability of Current SBMH Interventions

School: _____ SCG: _____ Recorder: _____ Date: _____

Name/Type of Intervention: _____

Question	Yes/No		Comments
1. Is the intervention choice determined by and meets school needs and connected with district goals and objectives?	Y	N	
2. Is there a clear and objective evaluation process with measures that relate to established district goals and school needs?	Y	N	
3. Is the intervention evidence-based?	Y	N	
4. Is the intervention up to date, or is there a newer evidence-based intervention available that meets the same school needs and district goals?	Y	N	
5. Is the intervention culturally sensitive?	Y	N	
6. Do the personnel delivering the intervention have appropriate training?	Y	N	
7. Are the costs to deliver the intervention reasonable (personnel, time, training costs, material costs)?	Y	N	
8. Does the intervention offer sufficient dosage (e.g., is the intervention duration long enough and frequent enough to be effective)?	Y	N	
9. Is the intervention easily accessible for participants (e.g., participant fees, location, duration, time of day/school year)?	Y	N	
10. Is the intervention well attended?	Y	N	
TOTAL Yes and No	Y: N:		

SISSM Framework Tool D-1: Planning SBMH Interventions

SISSM Framework Tool D-1: Planning SBMH Interventions

School: _____ SCG: _____ Recorder: _____ Date: _____

Column 1 SBMH Priority Need	Column 2 MTSS Tier	Column 3 Intervention Type or Program Name	Column 4 Personnel		Column 5 Intervention/ Program Recipients	Column 6 Intervention/Program Accountability Measures			
			4a School Personnel	4b CO Personnel		6a Alignment with School District Strategic Goal(s)	6b Progress Monitoring	6c Evaluation of Outcomes	6d Intervention/ Program Integrity/ Fidelity
	Tier 1 Mental health literacy and awareness and mental health promotion								
	Tier 2 Targeted prevention for students at risk and early identification and intervention for emerging mental health disorders								
	Tier 3 Intense intervention and chronic care for students with serious mental health disorders								

SISSM Framework Tool D-2: Determining Applicability of Potential SBMH Interventions

SISSM Framework Tool D-2: Determining Applicability of Potential SBMH Interventions

School: _____ SCG: _____ Recorder: _____ Date: _____

Name/Type of Intervention/Program: _____

Question	Yes/No (circle)		Comments
1. Is the intervention evidence-based?	Y	N	
2. Is the intervention culturally sensitive?	Y	N	
3. Does the intervention meet school needs and address district goals?	Y	N	
4. Does the intervention require extensive personnel training?	Y	N	
5. Are there sufficient appropriately trained personnel available to deliver the intervention?	Y	N	
6. Are the costs to deliver the intervention reasonable (personnel, time, training costs, material costs)?	Y	N	
7. Does the intervention offer sufficient dosage (e.g., is the intervention duration long enough and frequent enough to be effective)?	Y	N	
8. Will the intervention be easily accessible for participants (e.g., participant fees, location, duration, time of day/school year)?	Y	N	
9. Does the intervention include a clear and objective evaluation process with measures that relate to established district goals?	Y	N	
TOTAL Yes and No	Y: N:		

References

Baker, J. A. (2008). Assessing school risk and protective factors. In B. Doll & J. A. Cummings (Eds.), *Transforming school mental health services: Population-based approaches to promoting the competency and wellness of children.* Thousand Oaks, CA: Corwin Press.

Berzin, S. C., & O'Connor, S. (2010). Educating today's school social workers: Are school social work courses responding to changing context? *Children & Schools, 32*(4), 237–249.

Canadian Paediatric Society. (2009). *Are we doing enough? A status report on Canadian public policy and child and youth health.* Ottawa, ON: Author.

Center for Mental Health in Schools at UCLA. (2012a). *Screening mental health problems in schools.* Los Angeles, CA: Author. Retrieved January 10, 2012, from http://smhp.psych.ucla.edu/pdfdocs/policyissues/mhscreeningissues.pdf

Center for Mental Health in Schools at UCLA. (2012b). *A resource aid packet on addressing barriers to learning: A set of surveys to map what a school has and what it needs.* Los Angeles, CA: Author. Retrieved February 14, 2012, from http://smhp.psych.ucla.edu/pdfdocs/policyissues/mhscreeningissues.pdf

Center for Mental Health in Schools at UCLA. (2011). *Enhancing school staff understanding of mental health and psychosocial concerns.* Los Angeles, CA: Author. Retrieved November 23, 2011, from http://smhp.psych.ucla.edu/pdfdocs/enhancingschoolstaff.pdf

Charvat, J. L. (2005). NASP study: How many school psychologists are there? *Communiqué, 33*(6), 12–14. Retrieved July 28, 2009, from http://www.nasponline.org/publications/cq/cq336numsp.aspx

Crisp, H. L., Gudmundsen, G. R., & Shirk, S. R. (2006). Transporting evidence-based therapy for adolescent depression to the school setting. *Education and Treatment of Children, 29*(2), 287–309.

Cummings, J. A., & Doll, B. (2008). Getting from here to there. In B. Doll & J. A. Cummings (Eds.), *Transforming school mental health services: Population-based approaches to promoting the competency and wellness of children.* Thousand Oaks, CA: Corwin Press.

Domitrovich, C. E., Bradshaw, C. P., Greenberg, M. T., Embry, D., Poduska, J. M., & Ialongo, N. (2009). Integrated models of school-based prevention: The logic and theory. *Psychology in the Schools, 47*(1), 71–88.

Elias, M. J., Zins, J. E., Graczyk, P. A., & Weissberg, R. (2003). Implementation, sustainability, and scaling up of social-emotional and academic innovations in public schools. *School Psychology Review, 32*(3), 303–319.

Ervin, R. A., & Schaughency, E. (2008). Best practices in accessing the systems change literature. In A. Thomas & J. Grimes (Eds.), *Best practices in school psychology V* (pp. 853–873). Bethesda, MD: National Association of School Psychologists.

Famularo, L. (2009). *Toward interagency collaboration: The role of children's cabinets.* Cambridge, MA: Rennie Center for Education Research and Policy.

Fixsen, D. L., Naoon, S. F., Blasé, K. A., Friedman, R. M., & Wallace, F. (2005). *Implementation research: A synthesis of the literature.* Tampa, FL: University of South Florida, Louis de la Parte Florida Mental Health Institute, The National Implementation Research Network (FMHI Publication #231).

Fullan, M. (2010). *All systems go: The change imperative for whole system reform.* Thousand Oaks, CA: Corwin Press.

Gelzheiser, L. M. (2009). Preparing for the future of school psychology: A special educator's view. *Journal of Educational & Psychological Consultation, 19*(3), 259–266.

Goodman, R., Ford, T., Simmons, H., Gatward, R., & Meltzer, H. (2000). Using the strengths and difficulties questionnaire (SDQ) to screen for child psychiatric disorders in a community sample. *British Journal of Psychiatry, 177*, 534–539.

Gould, M. S., Greenberg, T., Velting, D. M., & Shaffer, D. (2003). Youth suicide risk and prevention interventions: A review of the past 10 years. *Journal of the American Academy of Child & Adolescent Psychiatry, 42*(4), 386–405.

Government of Manitoba. (2012). *The Healthy Child Manitoba Act.* Retrieved June 2, 2012, from http://web2.gov.mb.ca/laws/statutes/ccsm/h037e.php

Hartigan, P. (2011). Integrated data systems link schools and communities. *Harvard Education Letter, 27*(4), 1–3.

Hunter, L., Hoagwood, K., Evans, S., Weist, M., Smith, C., Paternité, C., Horner, R., Osher, D., Jensen, P., & the School Mental Health Alliance (2005). *Working together to promote academic performance, social and emotional learning, and mental health for all children.* New York: Center for the Advancement of Children's Mental Health at Columbia University.

Jimerson, H. R., Stewart, K., Skokut, M., Cardenas, S., & Malone, H. How many school psychologists are there in each country of the world? International estimates of school psychologists and school psychologist-to-student ratios. Retrieved January 15, 2012, from http://education.ucsb.edu/jimerson/IISP/InternationalRatios_SPI2009.pdf

Kendall, P. C., Gosch, E., Furr, J. M., & Sood, E. (2008). Flexibility within fidelity. *Journal of the American Academy of Child & Adolescent Psychiatry, 47*(9), 987–993.

Kilkenny, R., Katz, N., & Baron, L. (2009). Leveraging mental health dollars into your district. *School Business Affairs,* July/August, 11–15.

Kratochwill, T. R., Volpiansky, P., Clements, M., & Ball, C. (2007). Professional development in implementing and sustaining multitier prevention models: Implications for response to intervention. *School Psychology Review, 36*(4), 618–631.

Kutash, K., Duchnowski, A. J., & Lynn, N. (2006). *School-based mental health: An empirical guide for decision makers.* Tampa, FL: The Research and Training Centre for Children's Mental Health, Louis de la Parte Florida Mental Health Institute, University of South Florida.

Lean, D. S., & Colucci, V. A. (2010). *Barriers to learning: The case for integrated mental health services in schools.* Lanham, MD: Rowman & Littlefield Education.

LeBuffe, P. A., Shapiro, V. B., & Naglieri, J. A. (2009). *The Devereux student strengths assessment.* Lewisville, NC: Kaplan Press.

Lever, N. A., Stephan, S. H., Axelrod, J., & Weist, M. D. (2004). Fee-for-service revenue for school mental health through a partnership with an outpatient mental health center. *Journal of Public Health, 74*(3), 91–94.

Limbrick, P. (2012). *Horizontal teamwork in a vertical world.* Clifford, UK: Interconnections.

Massey, O. T., Armstrong, K., Boroughs, M., Henson, K., & McCash, L. (2005). Mental health services in schools: A qualitative analysis of challenges to implementation, operation and sustainability. *Psychology in the Schools, 42*(4), 361–372.

McEwan, K., & Goldner, E. M. (2001). *Accountability and performance indicators for mental health services and supports.* Ottawa, ON: Federal/Provincial/Territorial Advisory Network on Mental Health.

Mellin, E. A., Bronstein, L., Anderson-Butcher, D., Amorose, A. J., Ball, A., & Green, J. (2010). Measuring interprofessional team collaboration in expanded school mental health: Model refinement and scale development. *Journal of Interprofessional Care, 25*(4), 514–523.

Merrell, K. W. (2010). Social-emotional assets and resilience scales. Euguene, OR: University of Oregon.

Morrison, J. Q., Graden, J. L., & Barnett, D. W. (2009). Steps to evaluating a statewide internship program: Model, trainee, and student outcomes. *Psychology in the Schools*, *46*(10), 989–1005.

Nastasi, M. L., Hatzichristou, C., Jones, J. M., Schanding, G. R., & Yetter, G. (2010). Evidence on multicultural training in school psychology: Recommendations for future directions. *School Psychology Quarterly*, *25*(4), 249–278.

National Association of School Psychologists (2006). School psychology: A blueprint for training and practice III. Retrieved January 16, 2012, from http://www.nasponline.org/resources/blueprint/FinalBlueprintInteriors.pdf

National Association of School Psychologists. (2010). *NASP model for comprehensive and integrated school psychological services: Helping students and schools achieve their best.* Bethesda, MD: Author.

National Association of State Boards of Education. (2012). Retrieved January 16, 2012, from http://nasbe.org/healthy_schools/hs/bytopics.php?topicid=2160&catExpand=acdnbtm_catB

Office of the Provincial Auditor. (2008). Community services, child and youth mental health agencies, Chapter 3, Section 3.04.

Price, O. A., & Lear, J. G. (2008). *School mental health services for the 21st century: Lessons from the District of Columbia school mental health program.* Washington, DC: Center for Health and Health Care in Schools.

Reinke, W. M., Herman, K. C., Stormont, M., Brooks, C., & Darney, D. (2010). Training the next generation of school professionals to be prevention scientists: The Missouri Prevention Center model. *Psychology in the Schools, 47*(1), 101–110.

Ringeisen, H., Henderson, K., & Hoagwood, K. (2003). Context matters: Schools and the "research to practice gap" in children's mental health. *School Psychology Review, 33,* 408–416.

Rowling, L. (2007). School mental health: Politics, power and practice. *Advances in School Mental Health Promotion,* Inaugural Issue, 23–29.

Saklofske, D. H., Schwean, V. L., Bartell, R., Mureika, J. M. K., Andrews, J., Derevensky, J., & Janzen, H. L. (2007). School psychology in Canada: Past, present, and future perspectives. In T. Fagan & P. Wise (Eds.), *School psychology: Past, present, and future perspectives.* Bethesda, MD: National Association of School Psychologists.

Sanetti, L. M., & Kratochwill, T. R. (2011). Toward developing a science of treatment integrity: Introduction to the special series. *School Psychology Review, 38*(4), 445–459.

Sebian, J., Mettrick, J., Weiss, C., Stephan, S., Lever, N., & Weist, M. (2007, June). *Education and systems of care approaches: Solutions for educators and school mental health professionals.* Baltimore, MD: Center for School Mental Health Analysis and Action, Department of Psychiatry, University of Maryland School of Medicine.

Skalski, A. K., & Smith, M. J. (2006, September). Responding to the mental health needs of students. *Principal Leadership,* 12–15.

Stiegler, K. (2012). School Connectedness Checklist. Retrieved January 17, 2012, from www.schoolmentalhealth.org/.../School%20Connectedness%20Checklist.doc.

Sturm, R., Ringel, J. S., Stein, B. D., & Kapur, K. (2001). *Mental health care for youth: Who gets it? How much does it cost? Who pays? Where does the money go?* Santa Monica, CA: RAND Corporation. Retrieved November 7, 2011, from http://www.rand.org/pubs/research_briefs/RB4541

Sugai, G. (2012, July). Multitier support systems: Features and considerations. Paper presented at the International School Psychology Association Conference, Montreal, QC.

Thompson, S., with J. Maxwell & S. M. Stroick. (1999). *Moving forward on child and family policy: Governance and accountability issues.* CPRN Discussion Paper No. F 08. Ottawa: Canadian Policy Research Networks Inc.

Weist, M. D., Rubin, M., Moore, E., Adelsheim, S., & Wrobel, G. (2007). Mental health screening in schools. *Journal of School Health, 77*(2), 53–58.

Weist, M. D., Sander, M. A., Walrath, C., Link, B., Nabors, L. Adelsheim, S., Moore, E., Jennings, J., & Carrillo, K. (2005). Developing principles for best practice in expanded school mental health, *Journal of Youth and Adolescence, 34*(1), 7–13.

Weist, M. D., Steigler, K., Stephan, S., Cox, J., & Vaughan, C. (2009). School mental health and prevention science in the Baltimore City Schools. *Psychology in the Schools, 47*(1), 89–100.

Welsh Government. (2012). National Service Framework for Children, Young People and Maternity Services. Retrieved June 11, 2012, from http://wales.gov.uk/topics/childrenyoungpeople/publications/nsfchildrenyoungpeoplematernity/?lang=en

Wingspread Declaration on School Connectedness. (2004, September). *Journal of School Health, 74*(7), 233–245.